a photo journal

AIRPORT

robert ornig

"DID YOU EVER NOTICE THAT
THE FIRST PIECE OF LUGGAGE
ON THE CAROUSEL NEVER
BELONGS TO ANYONE?"
ERMA BOMBECK

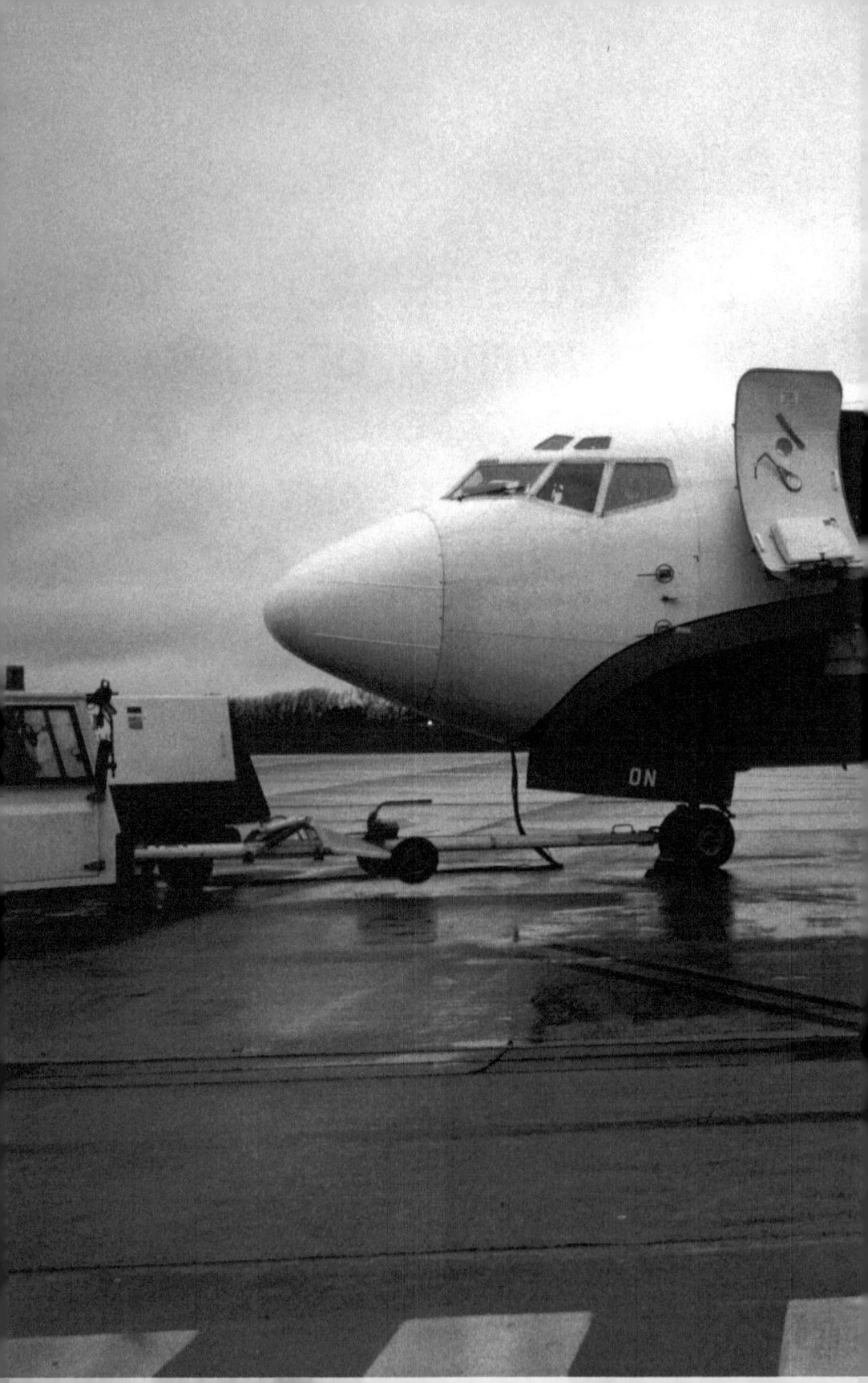

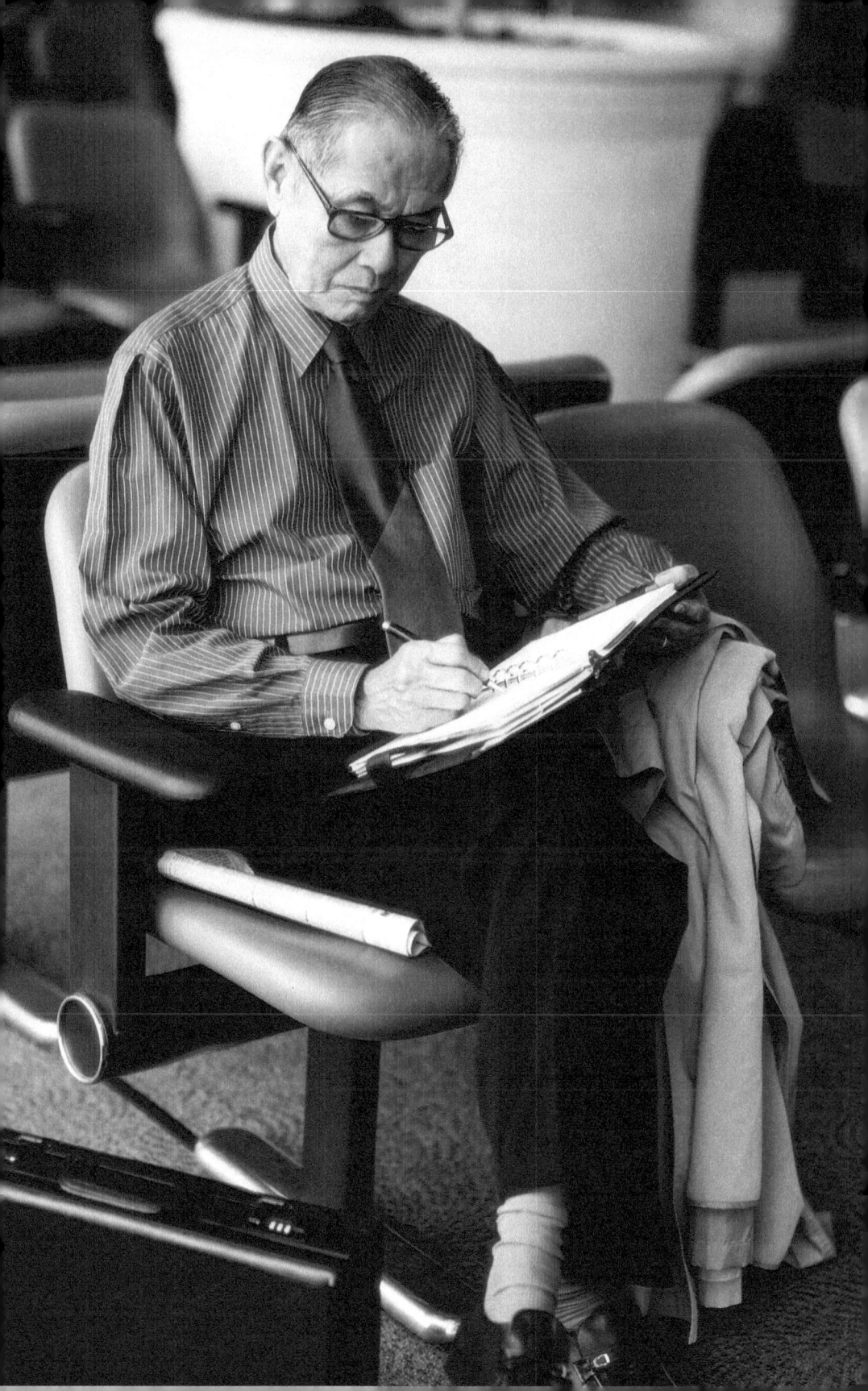

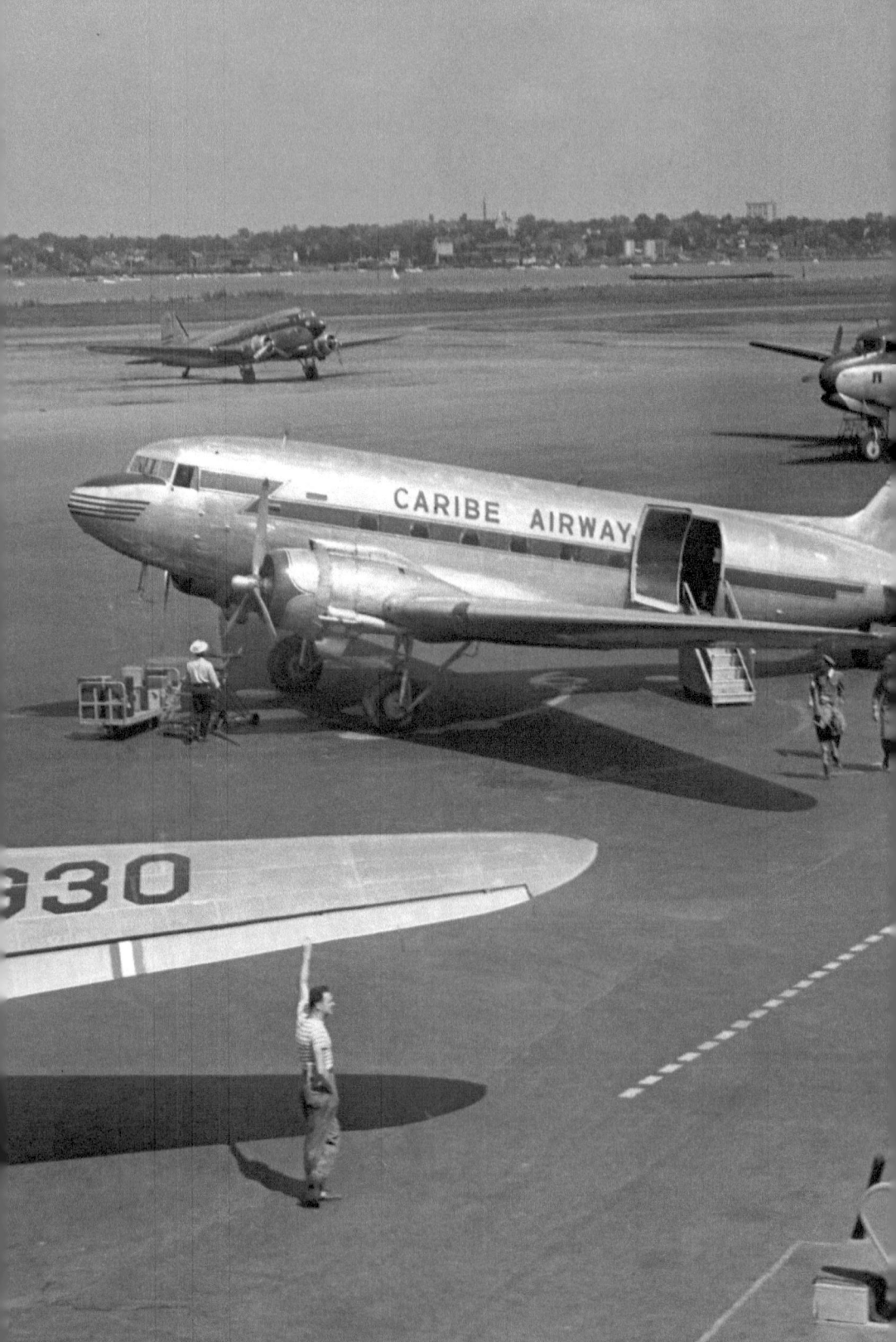

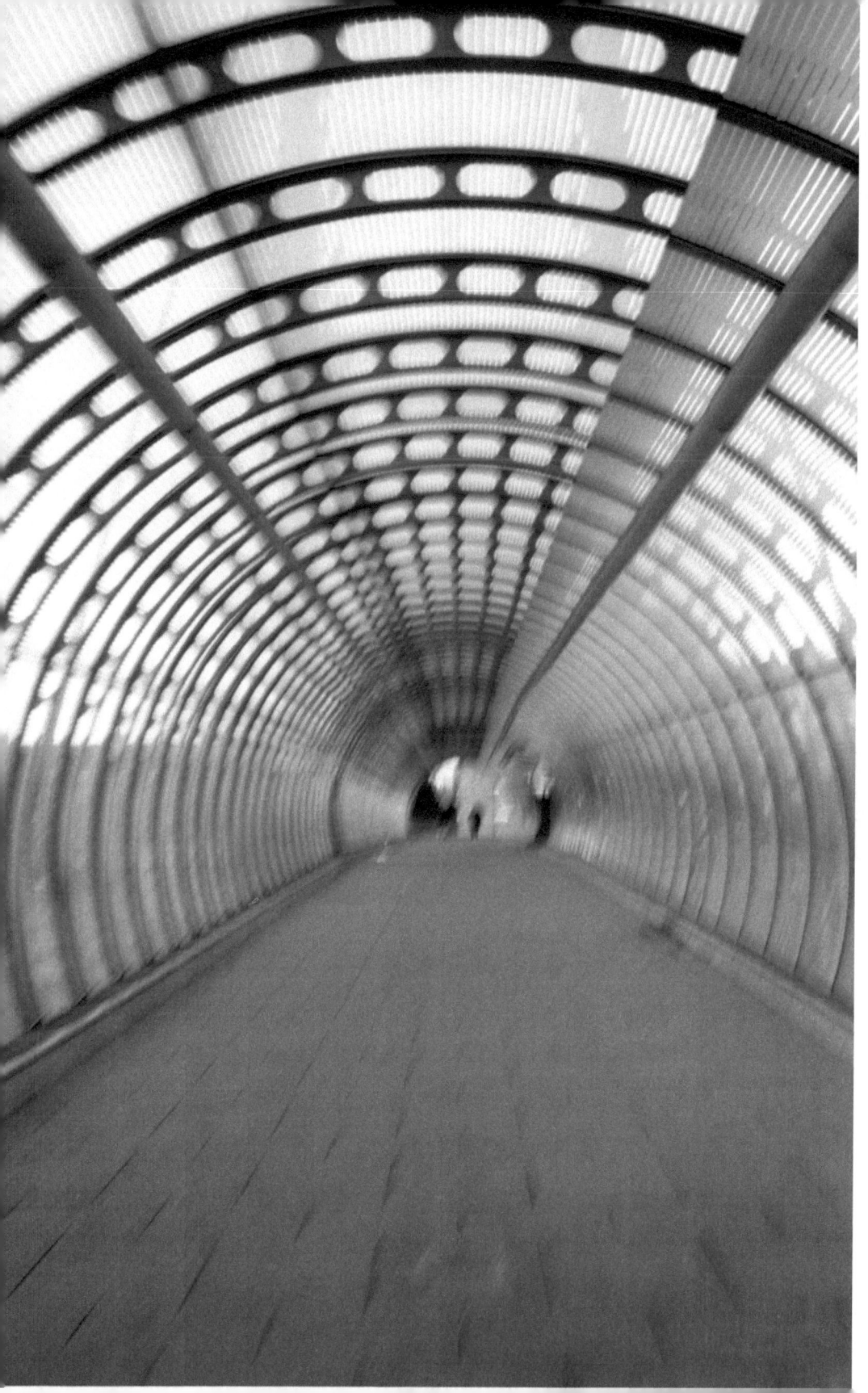

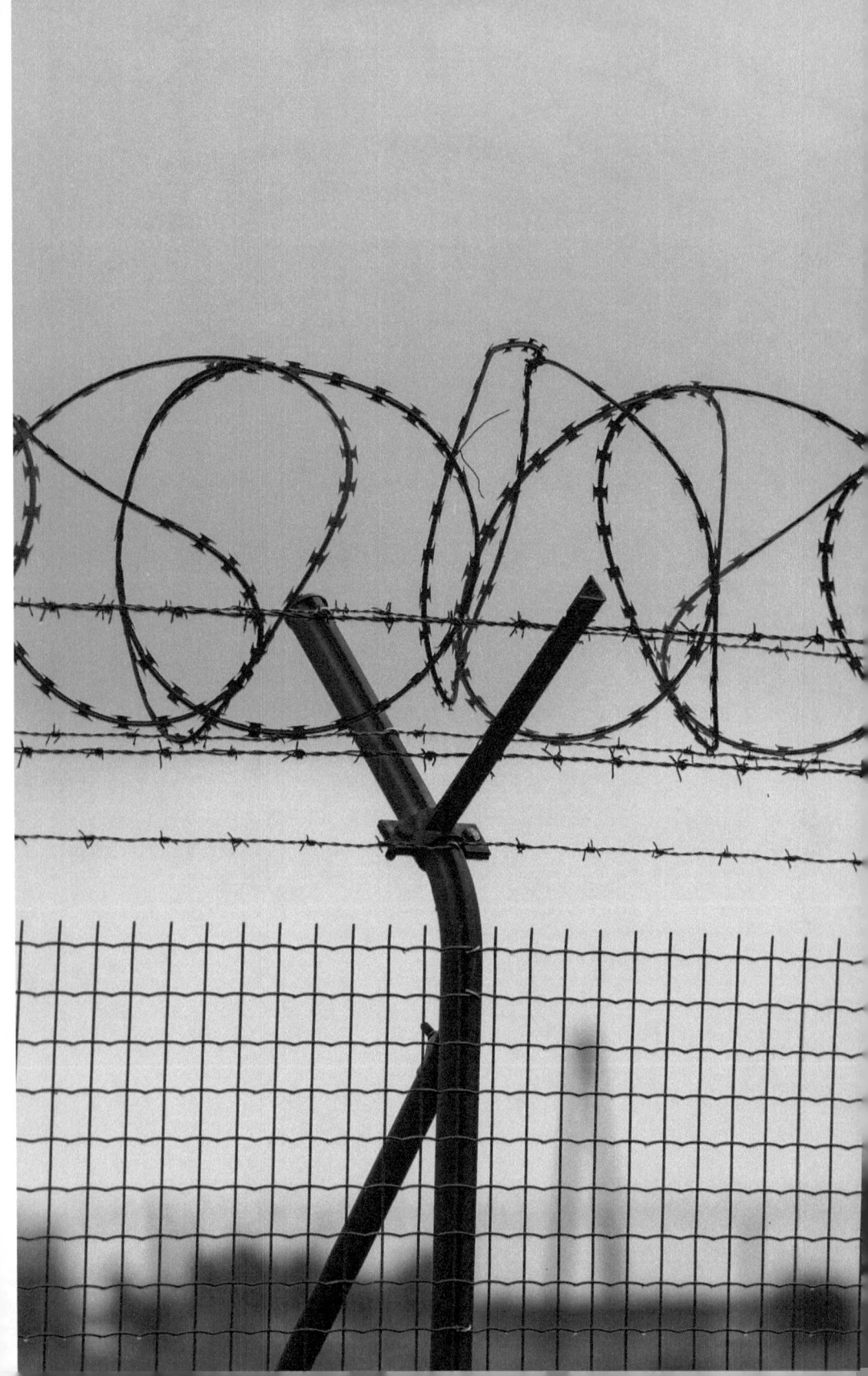

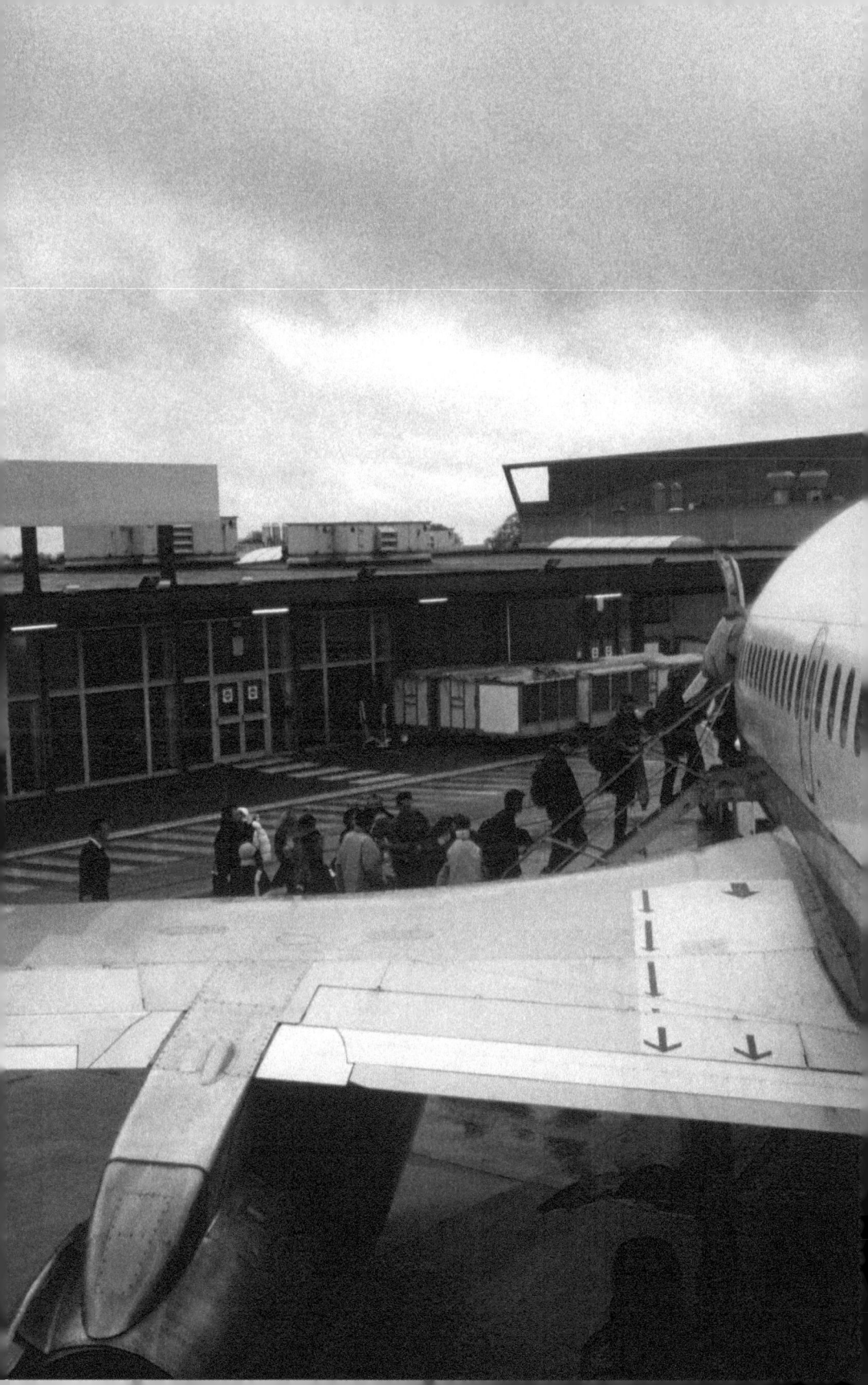

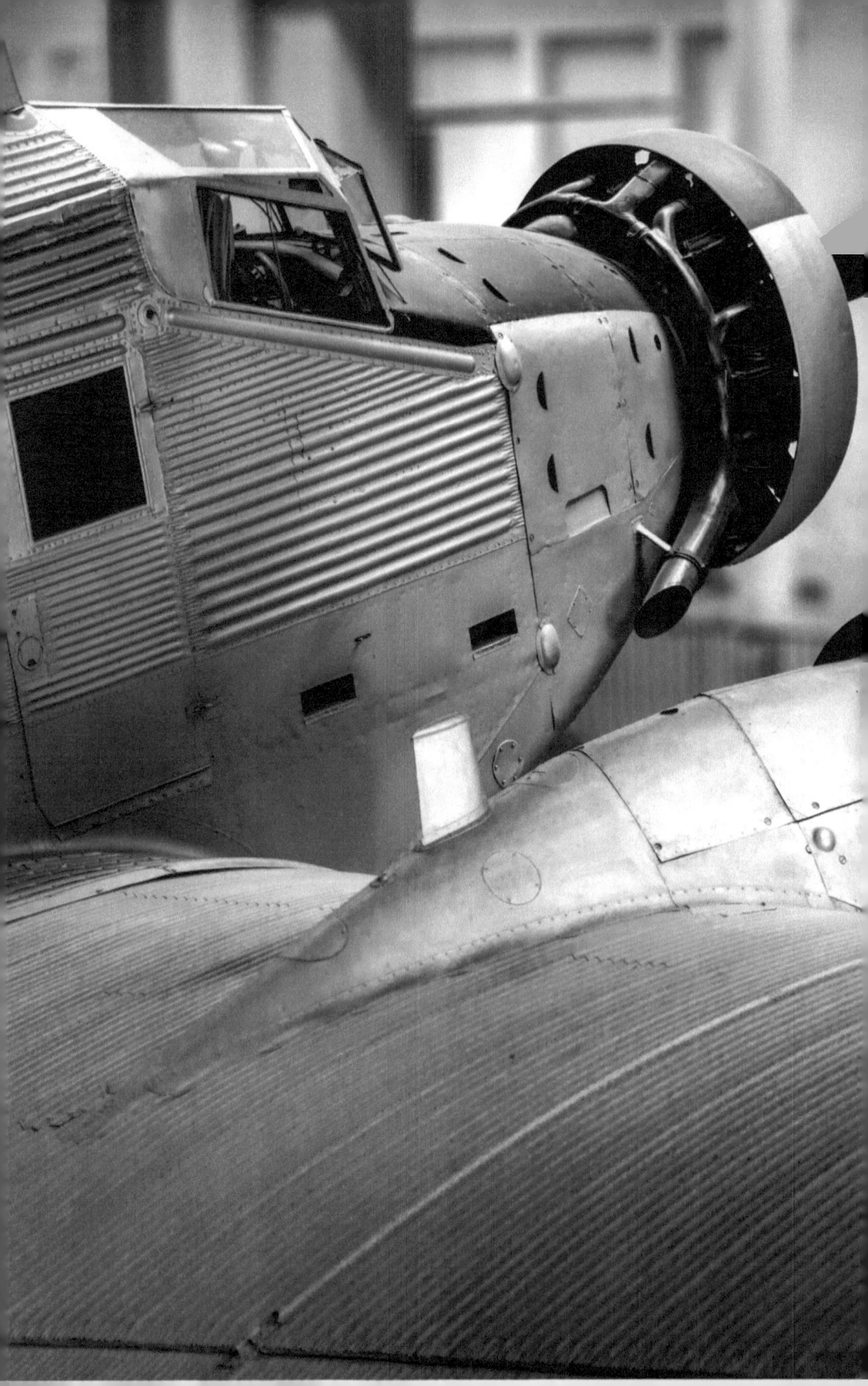

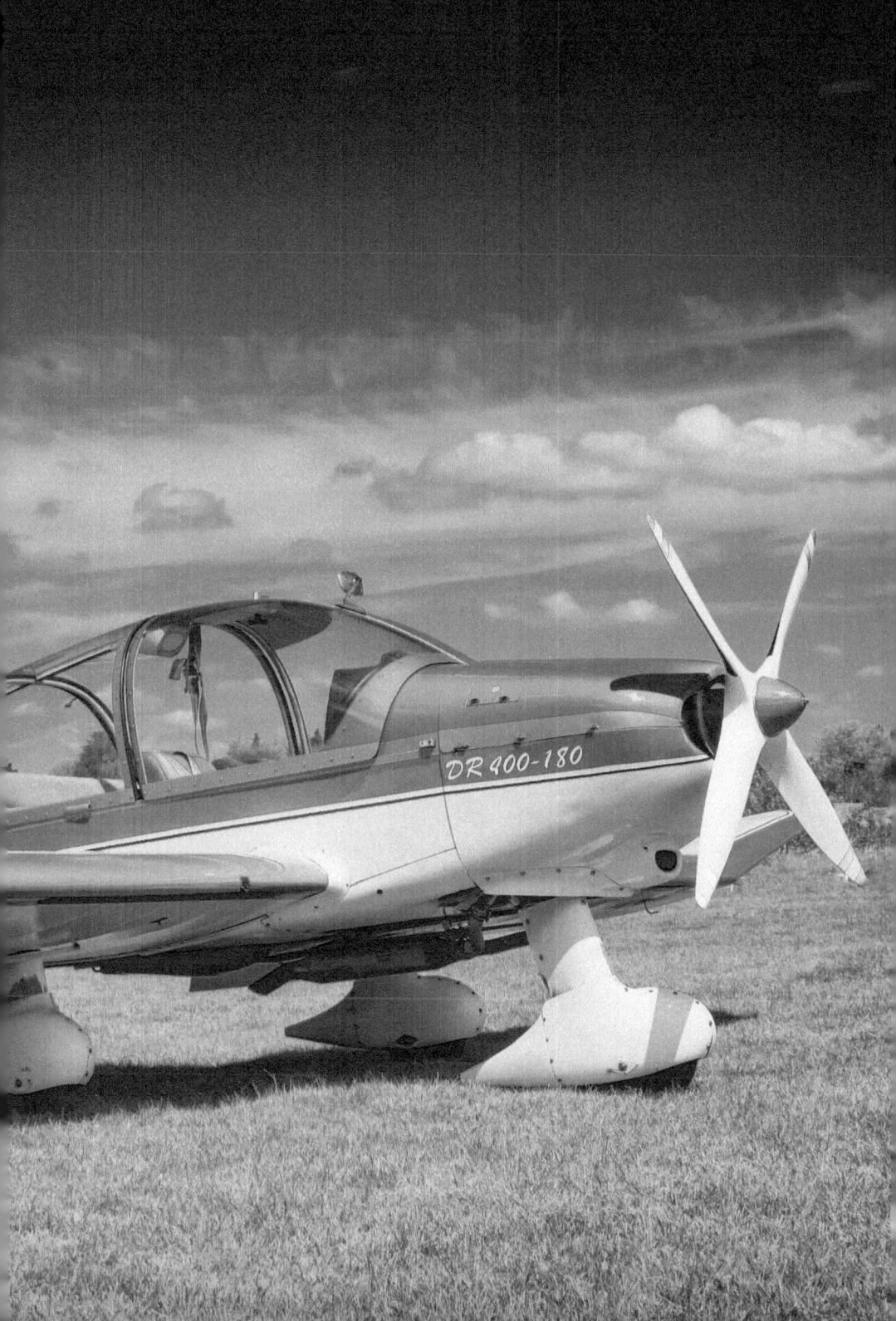

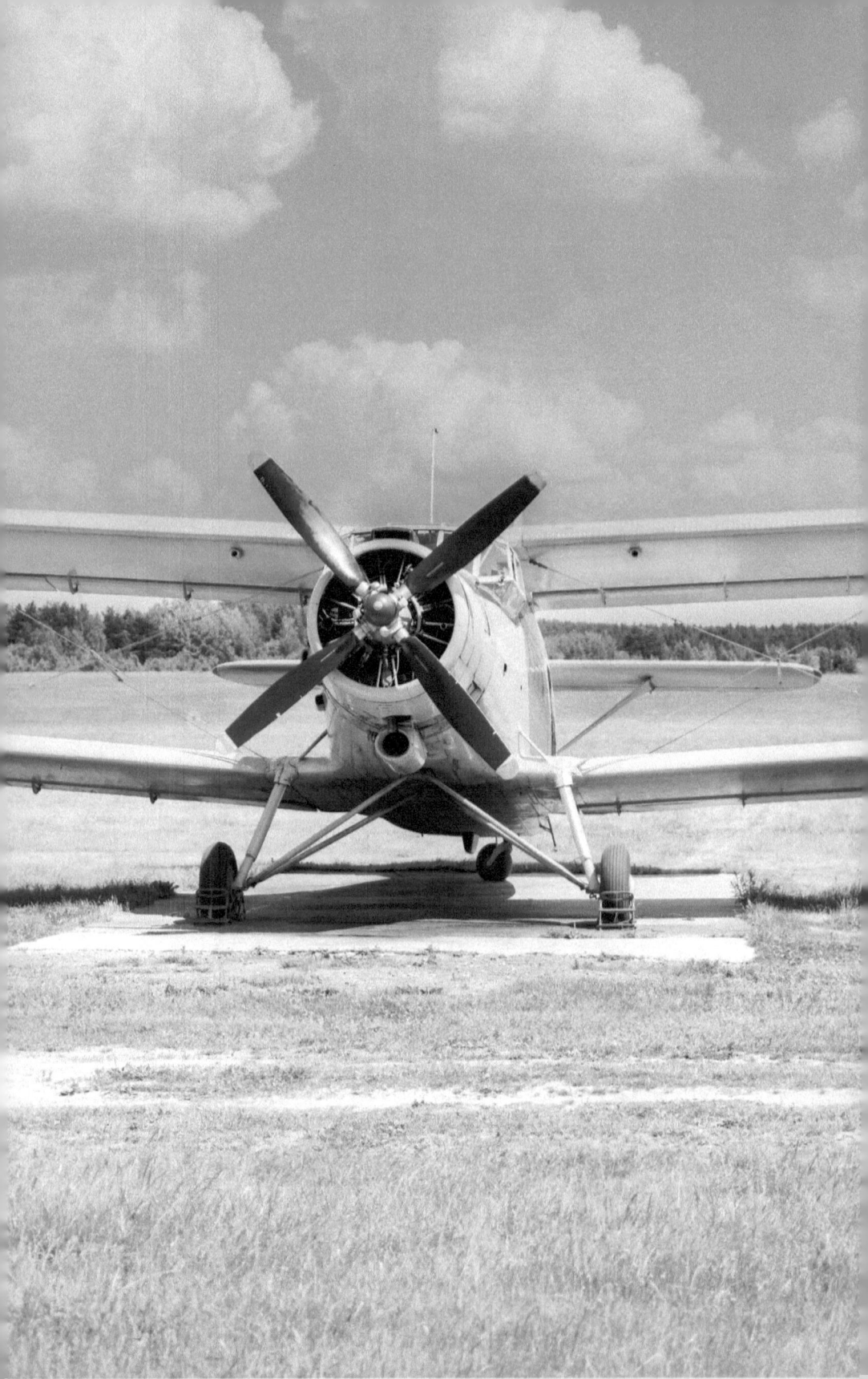

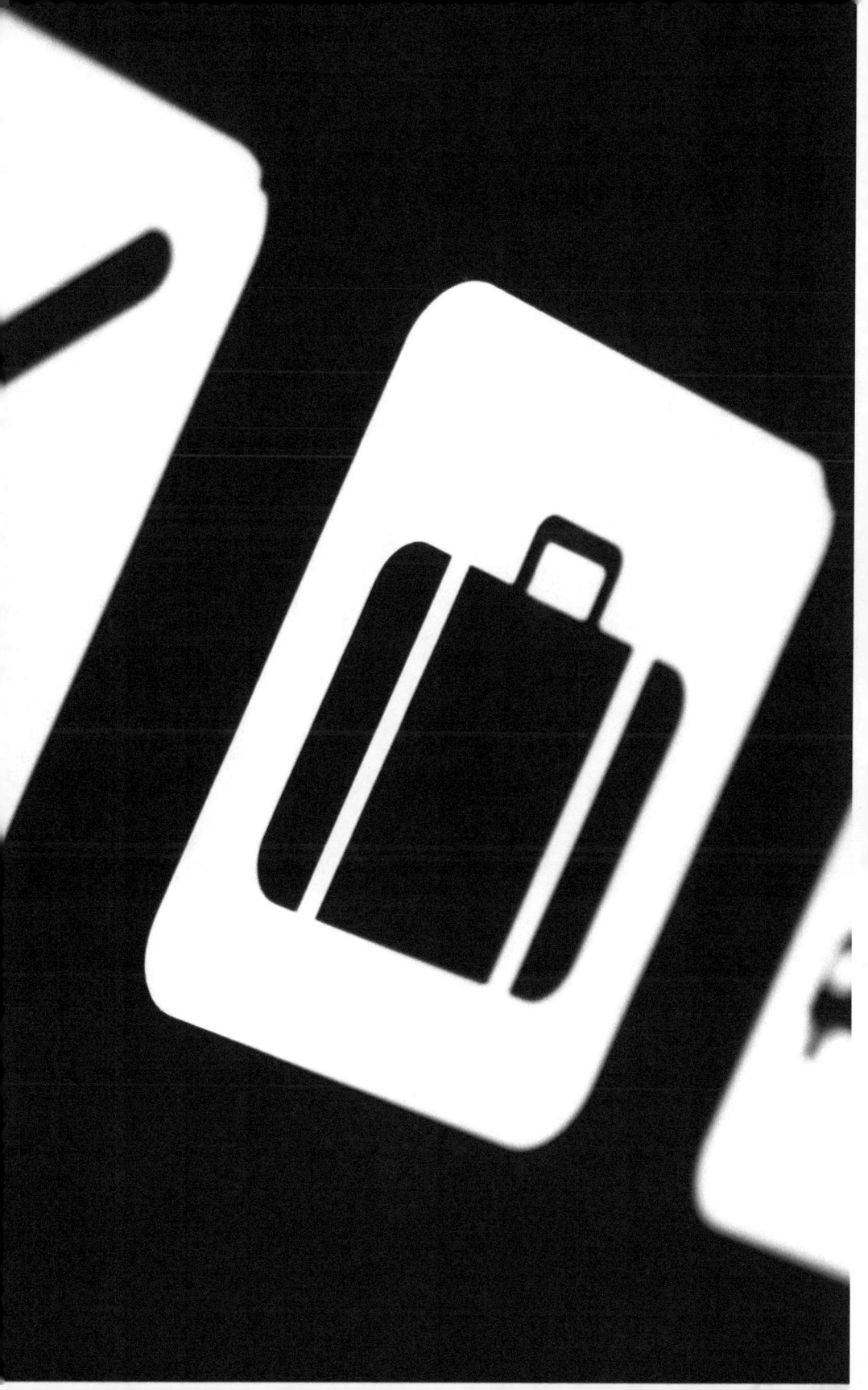

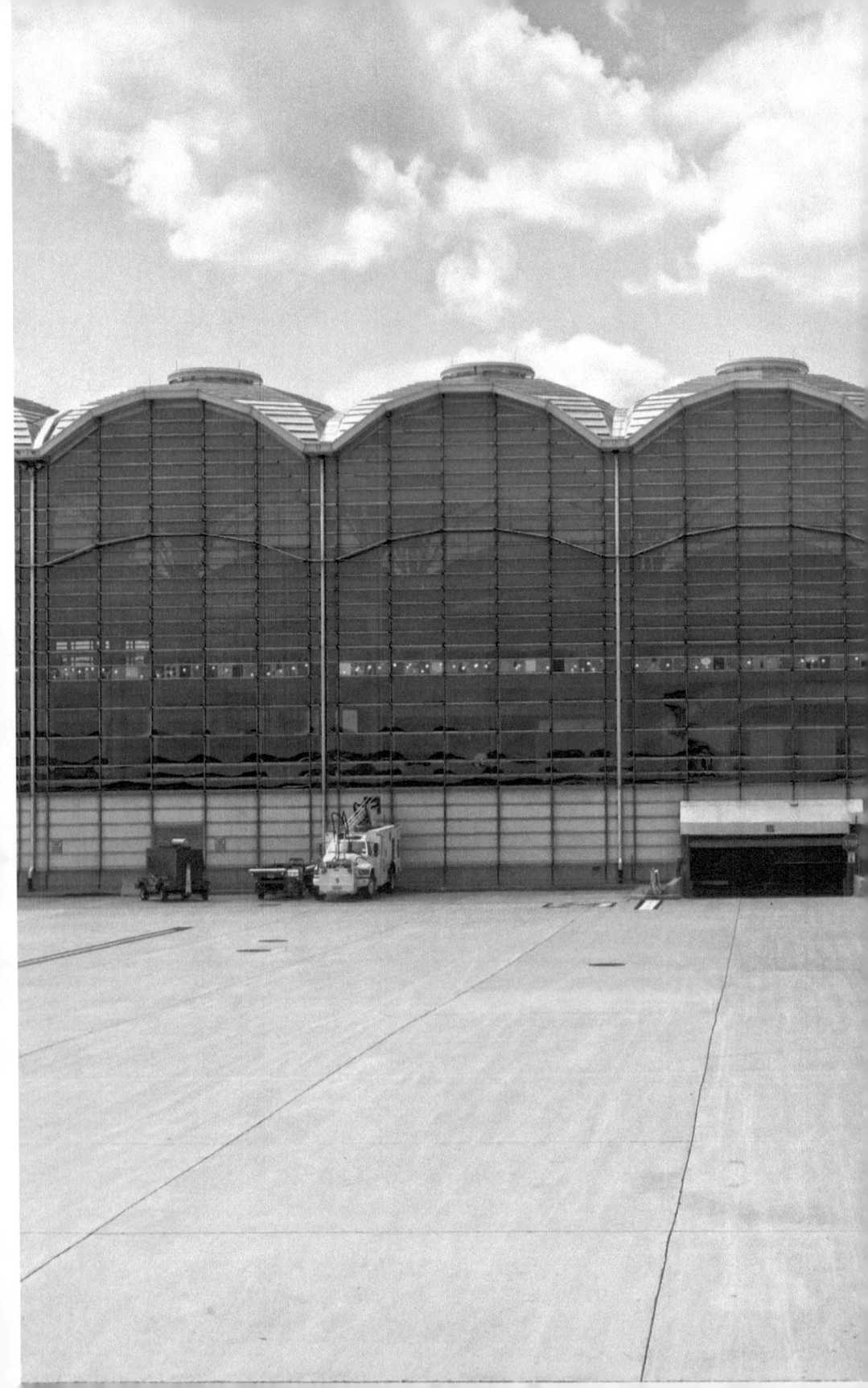

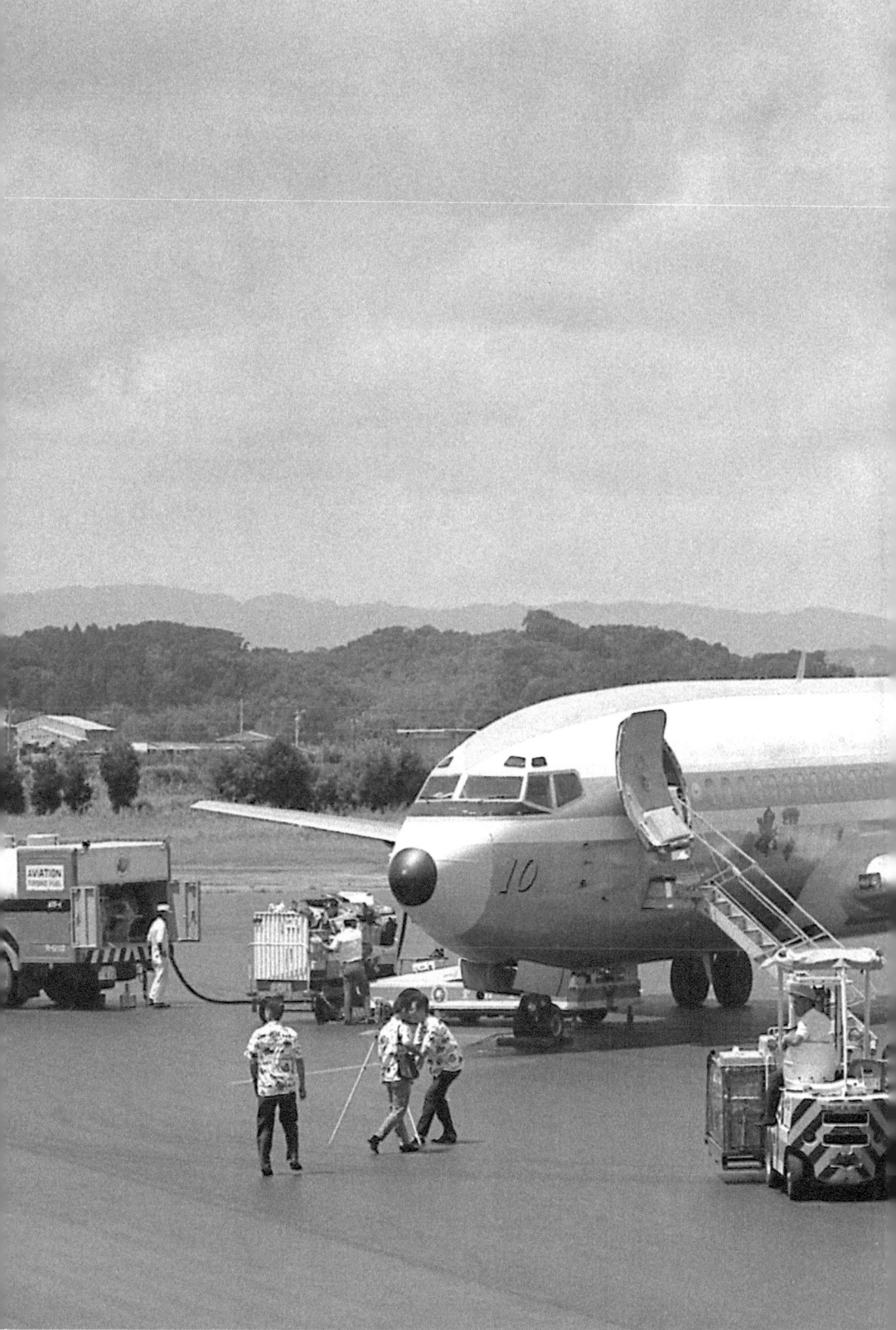

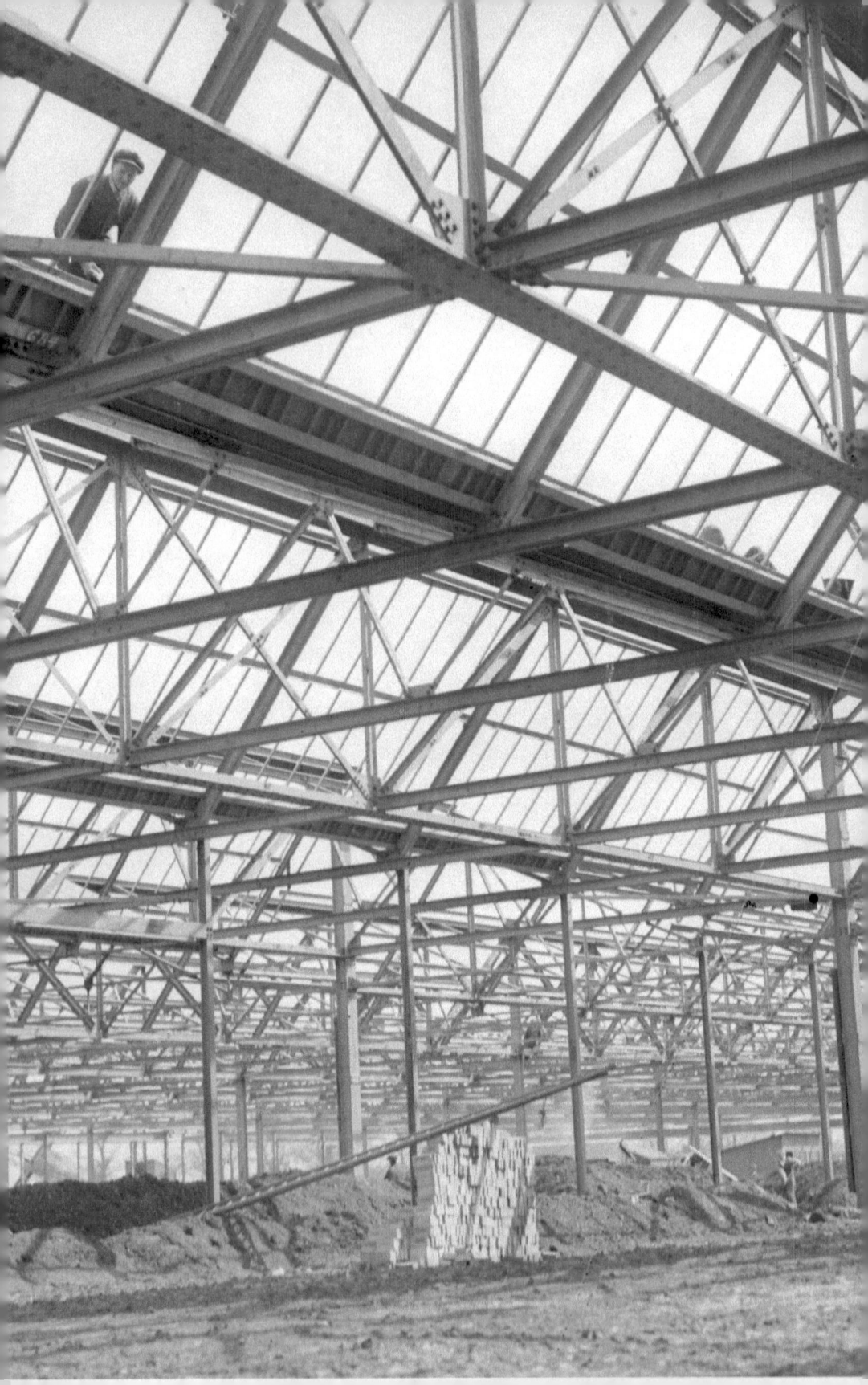

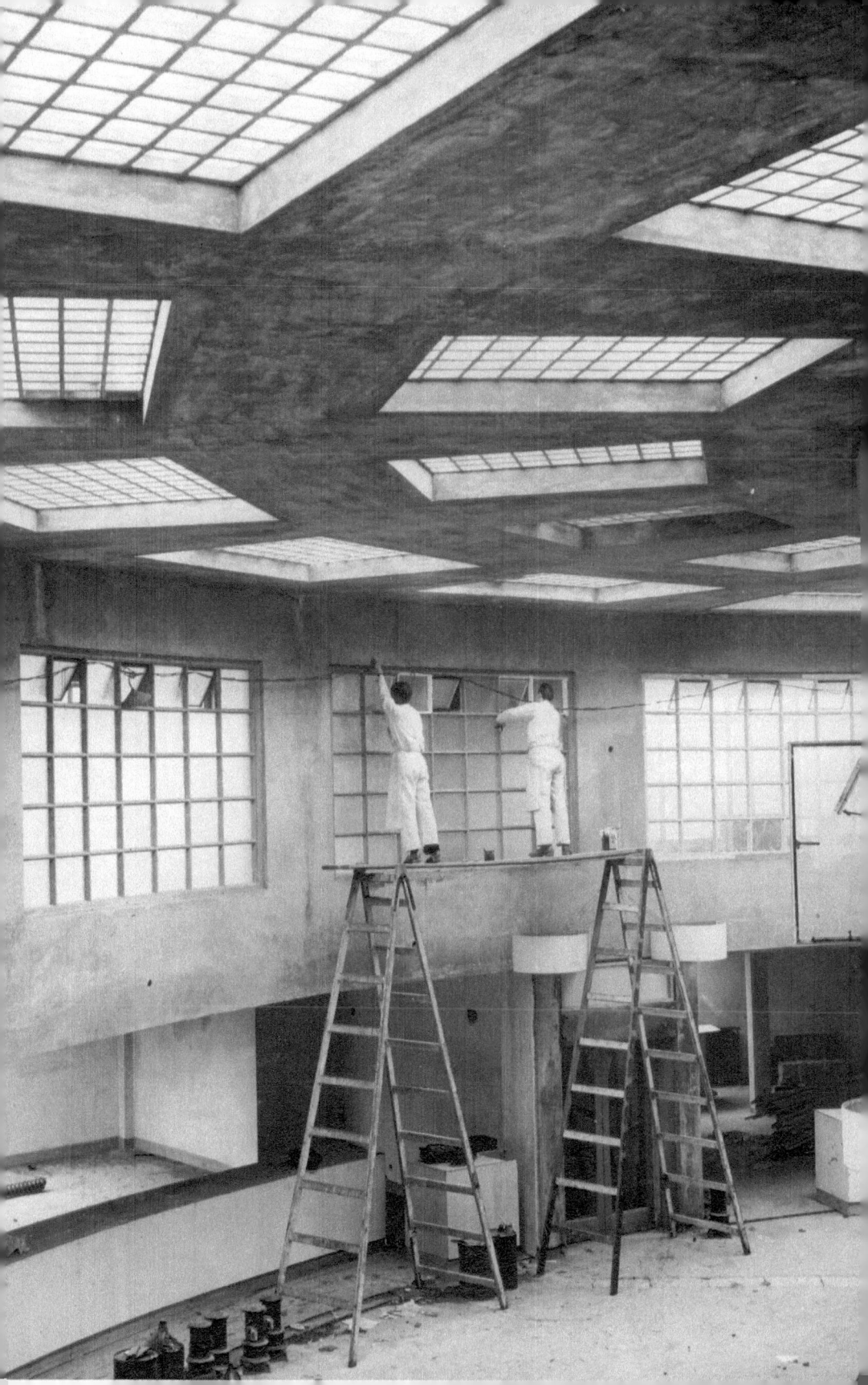

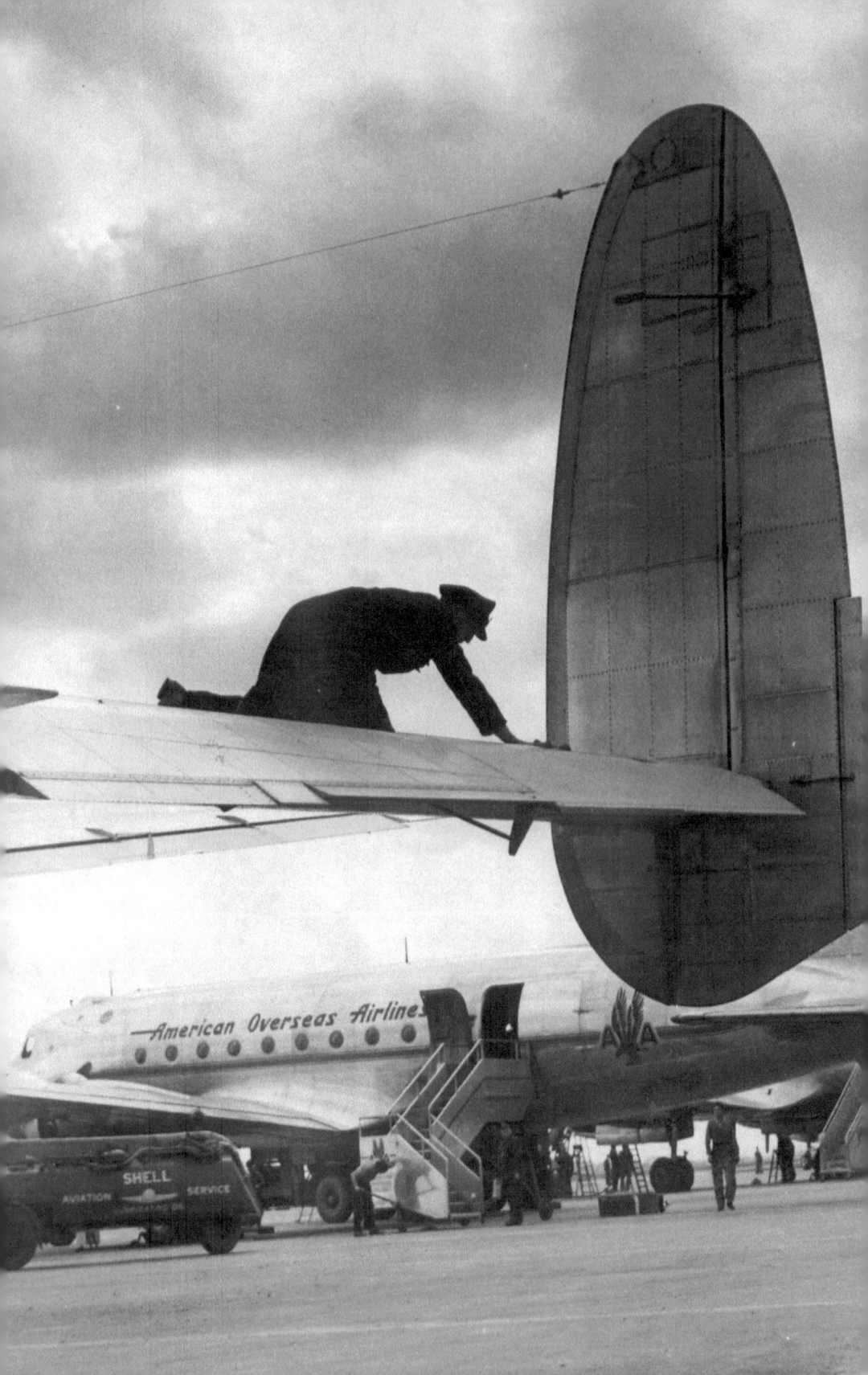

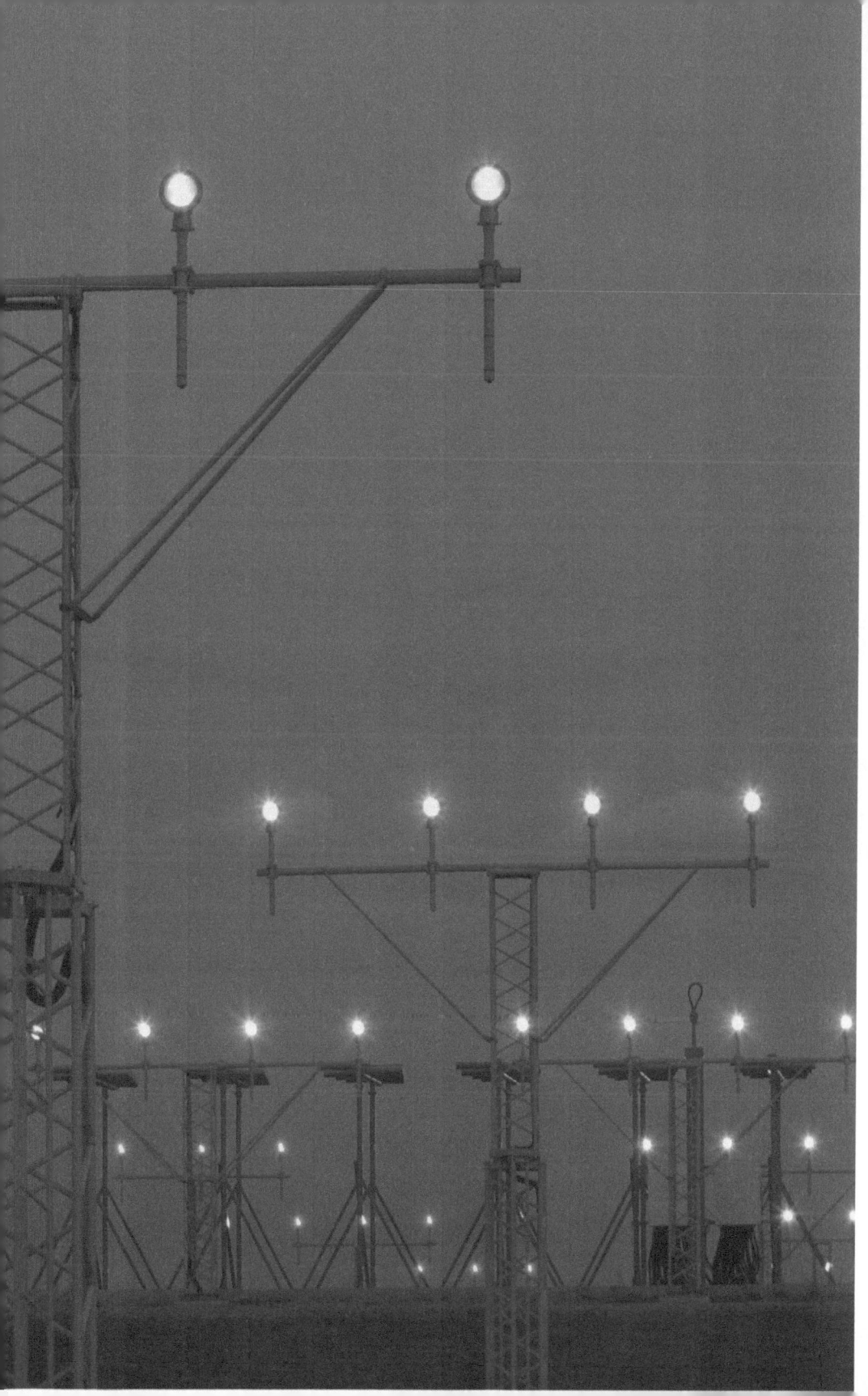

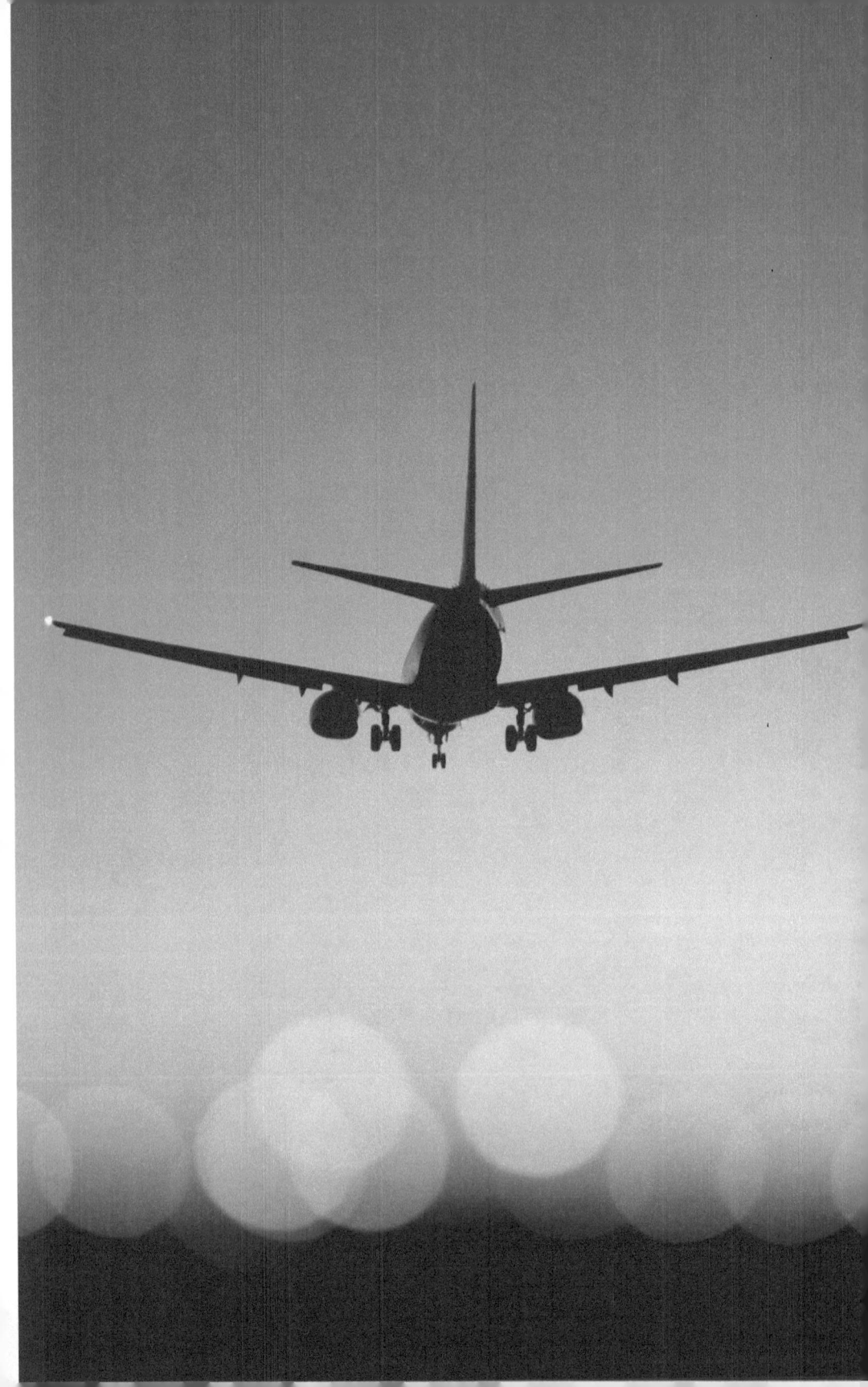

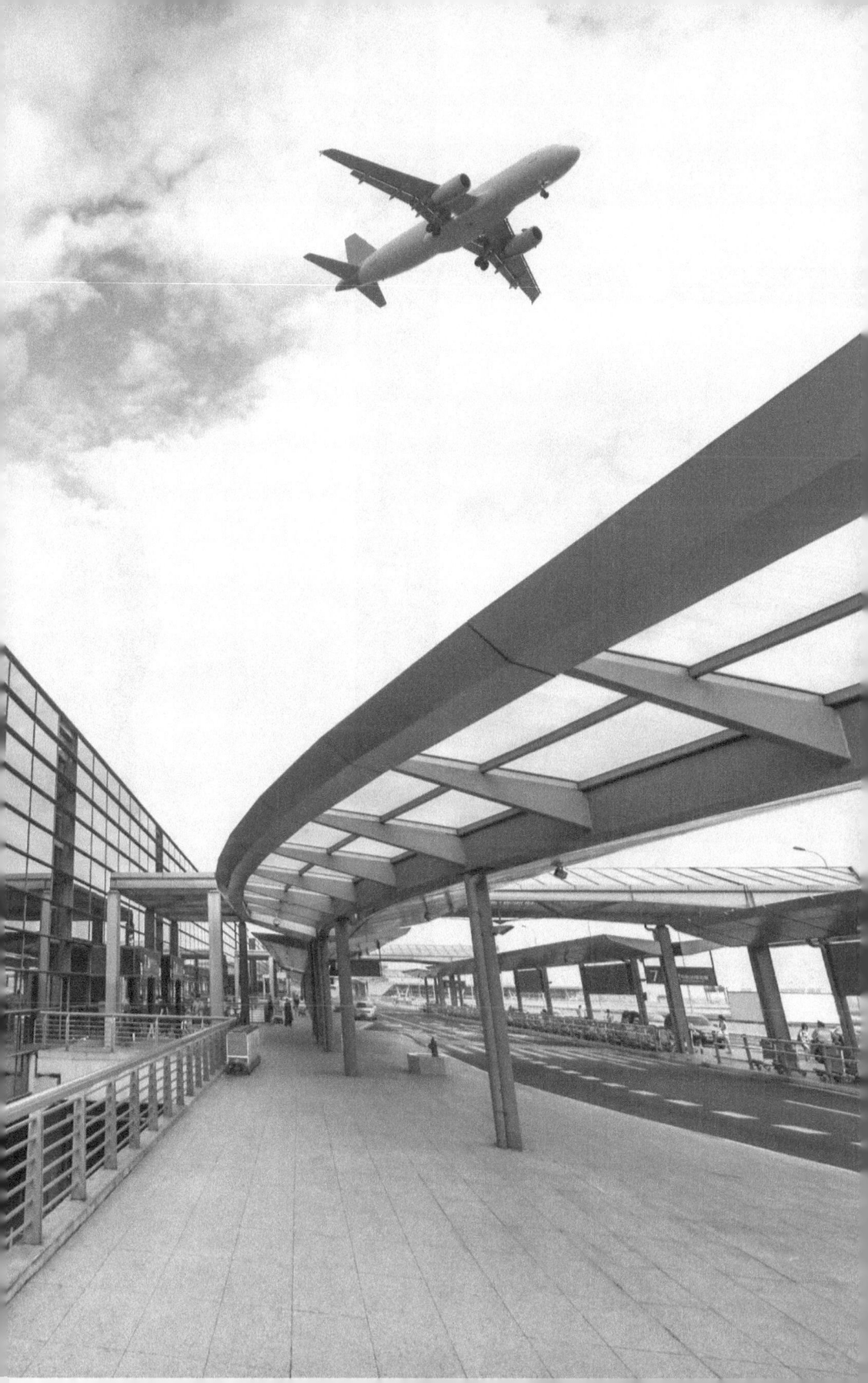

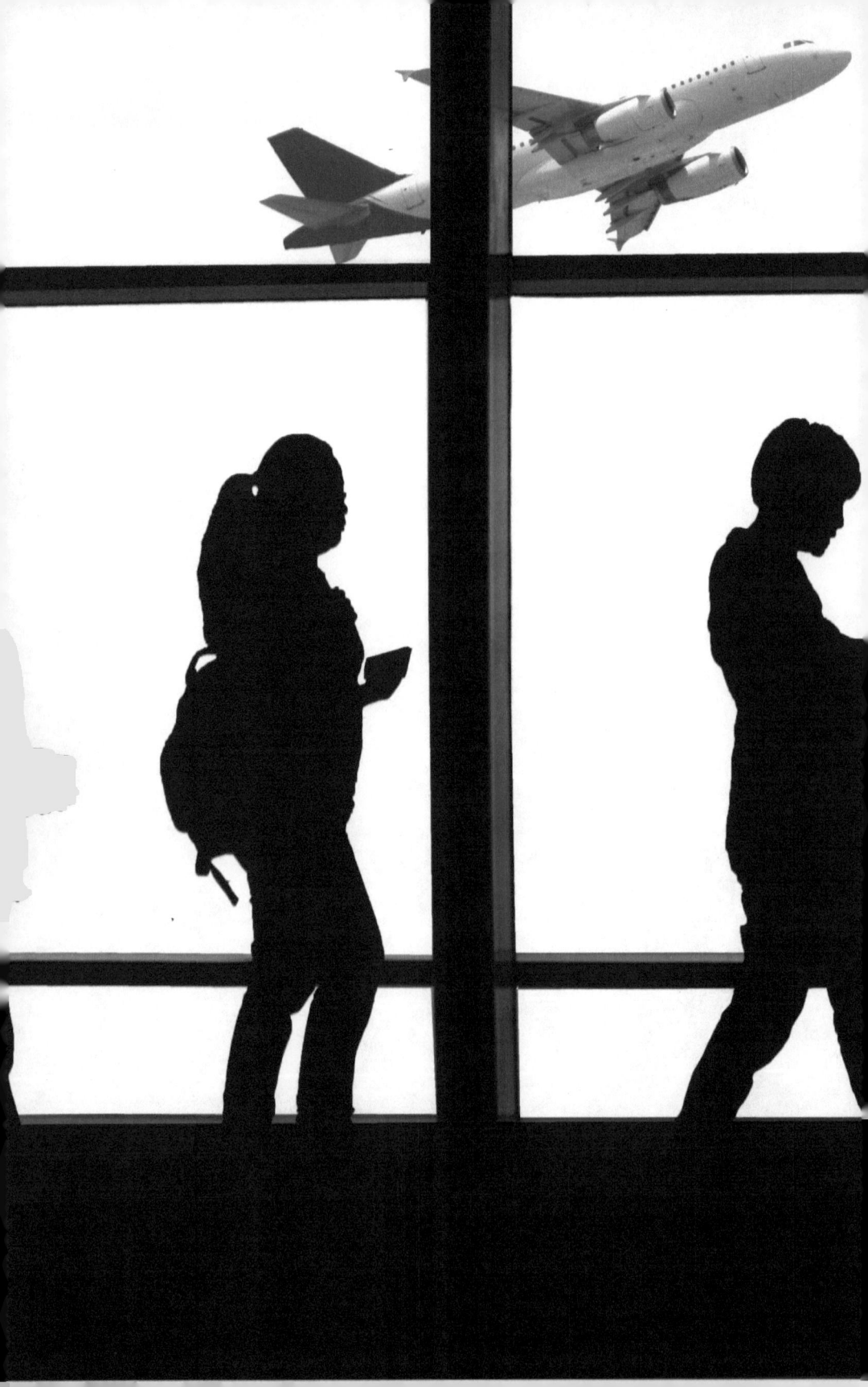

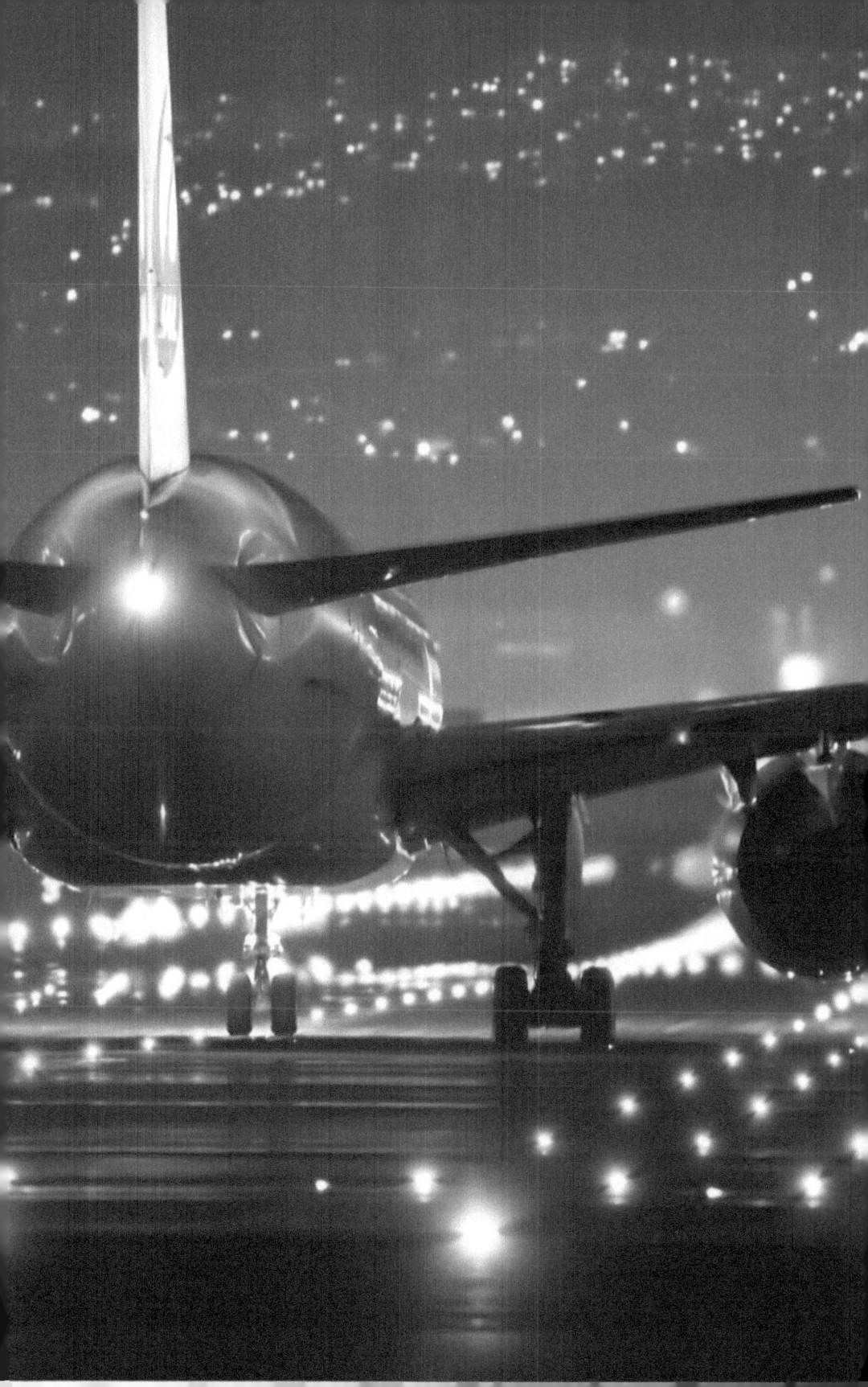

ENCHEN

RLIN-TEGEL

RANKFURT

UDAPEST

ARIS-CDG

STANBUL

URGHADA

ZMIR

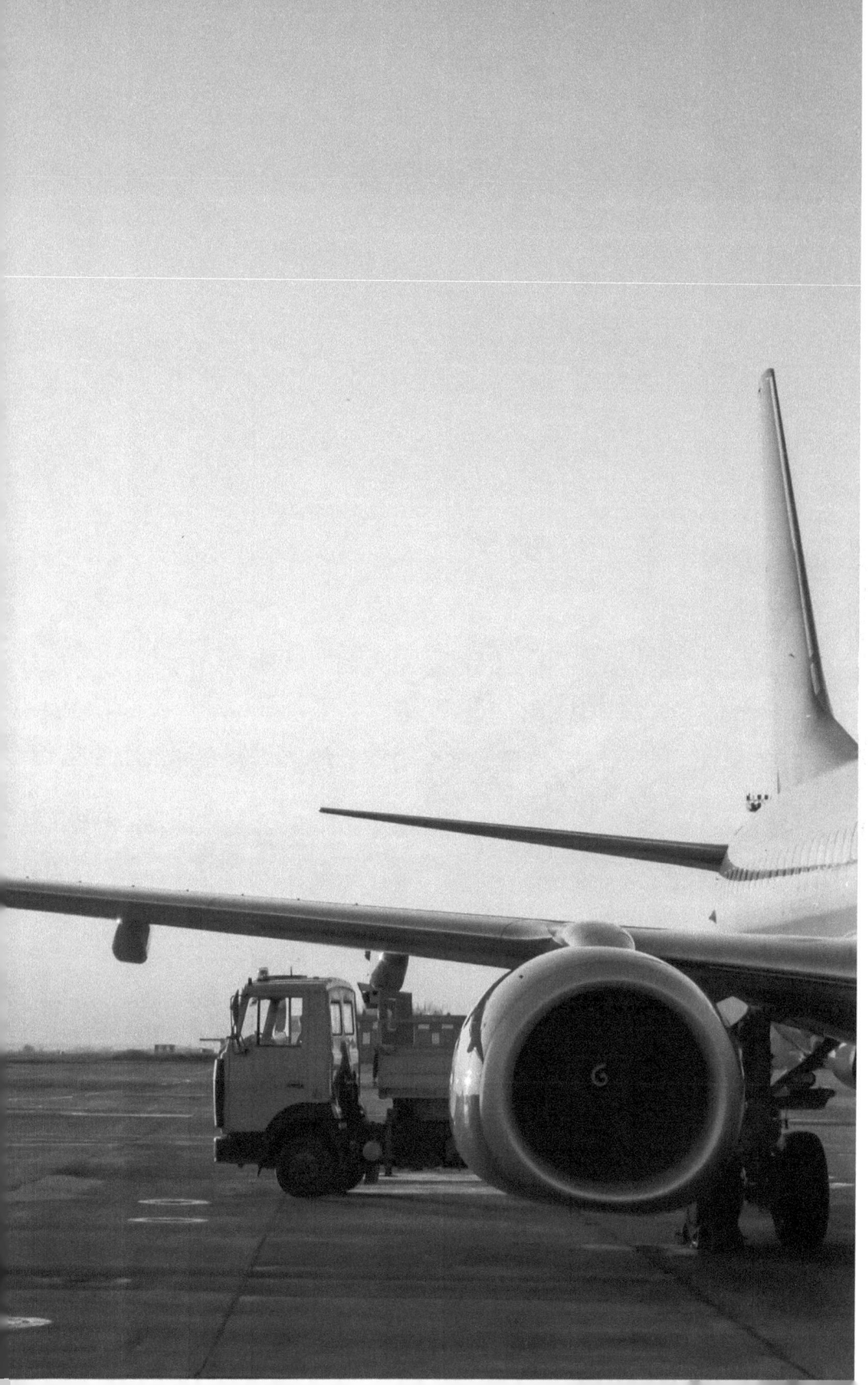

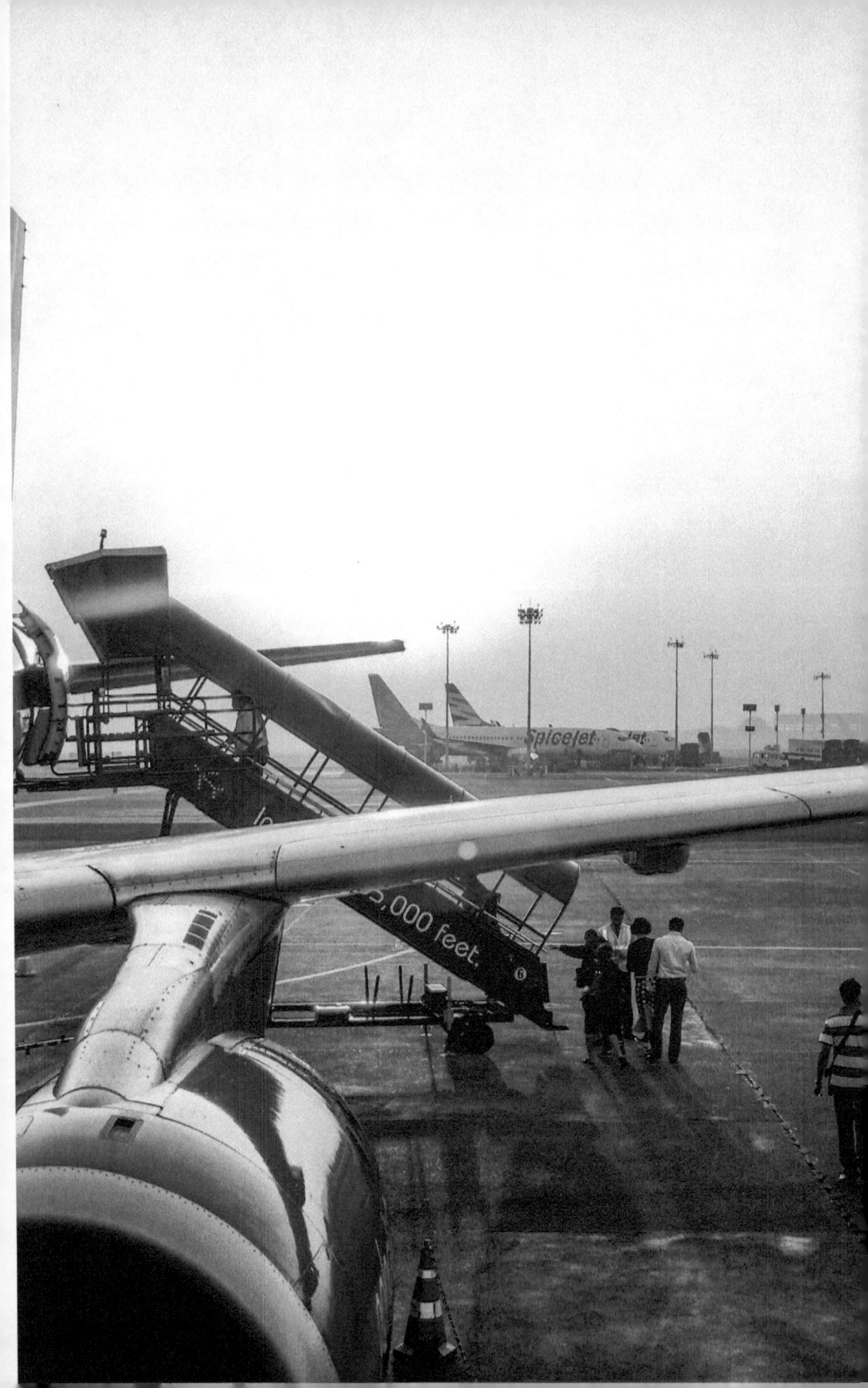

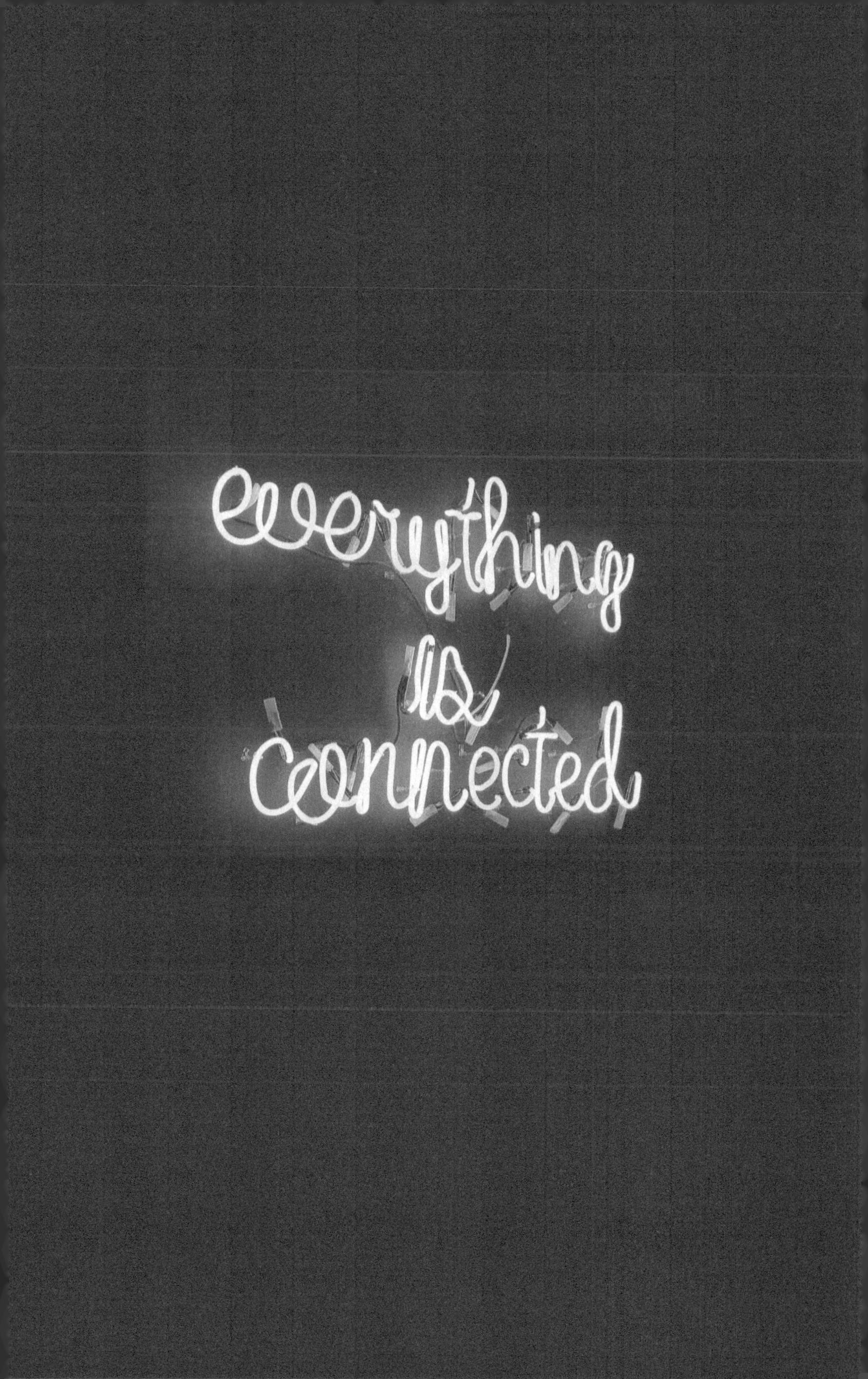
everything
is
connected

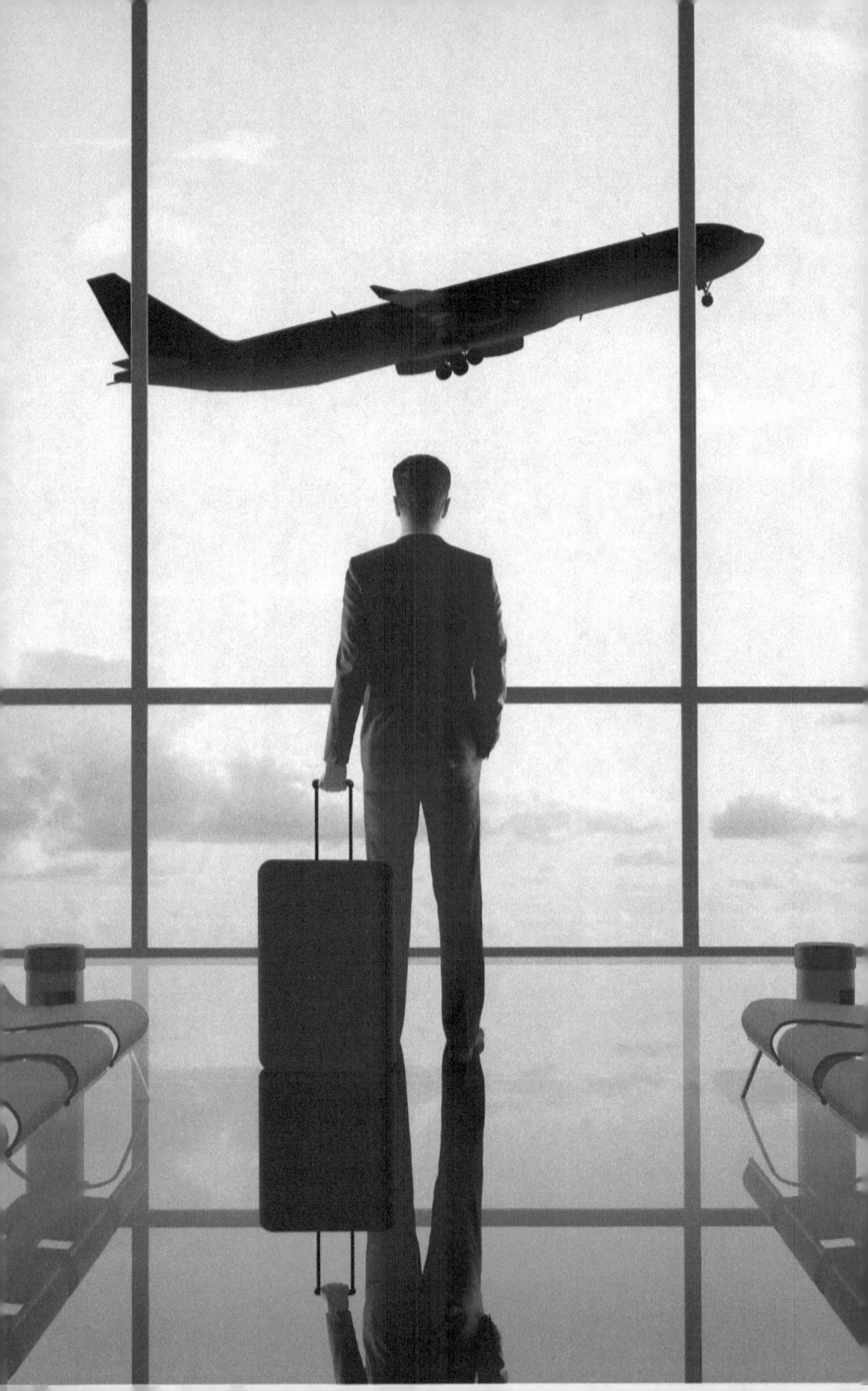

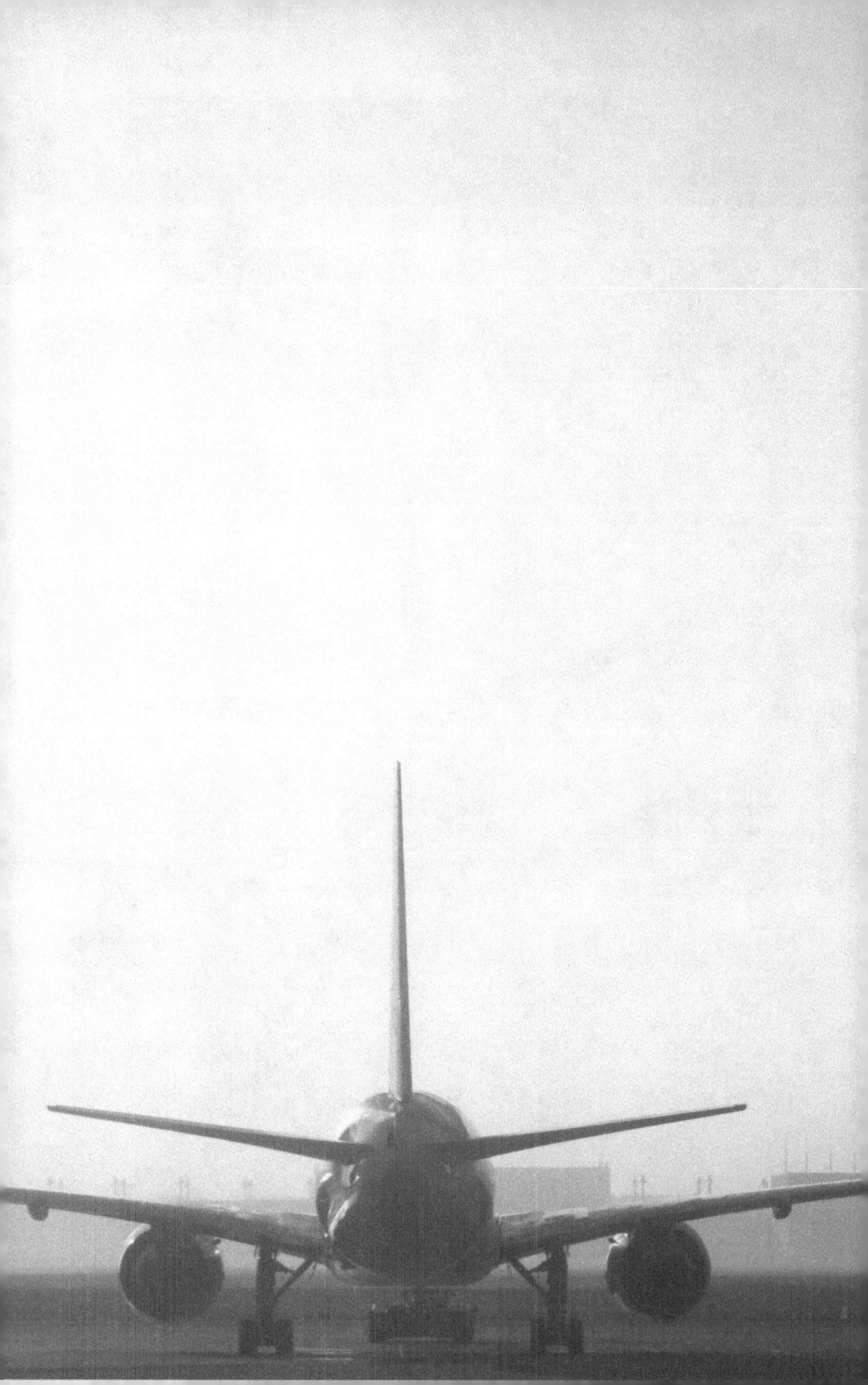

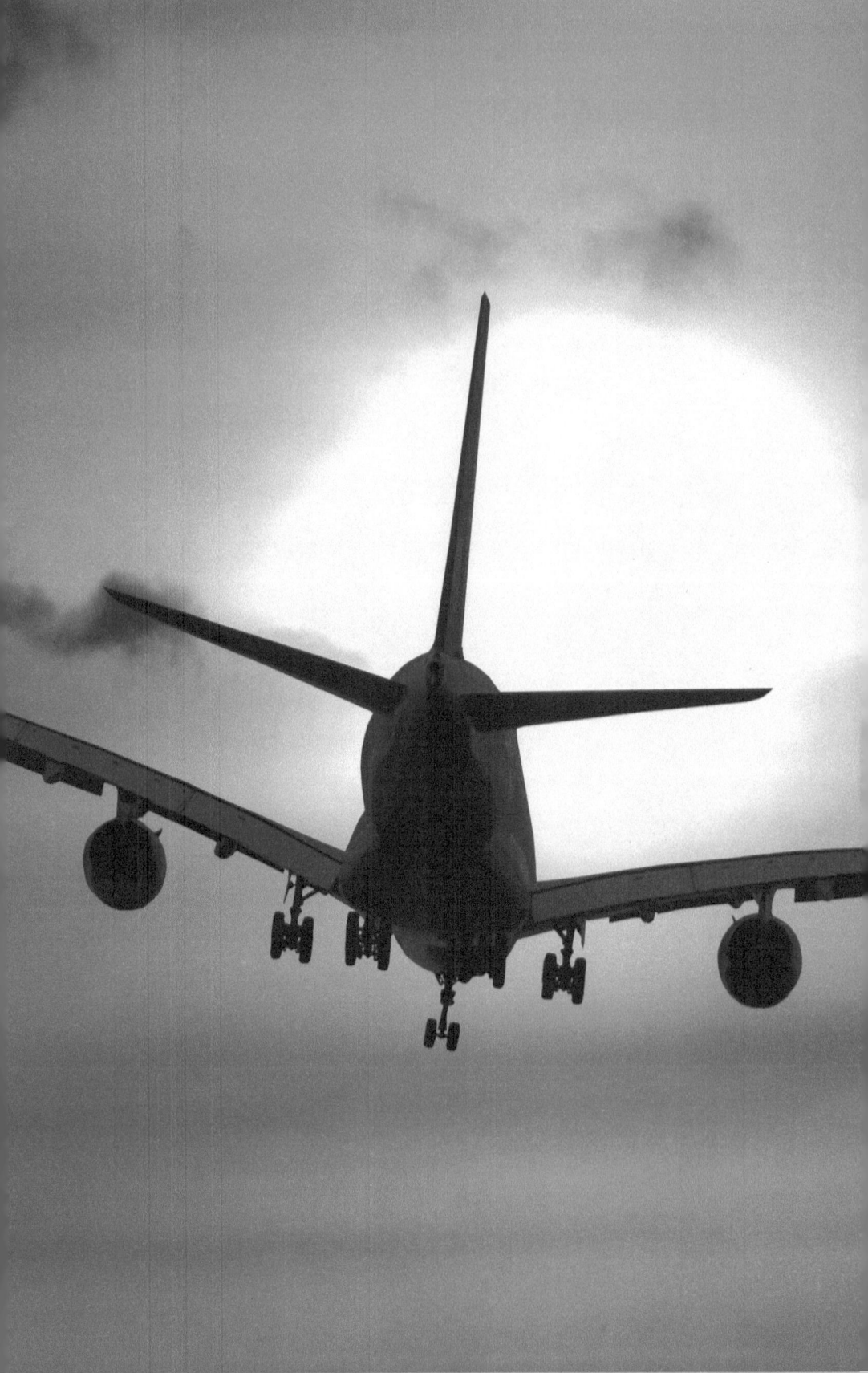

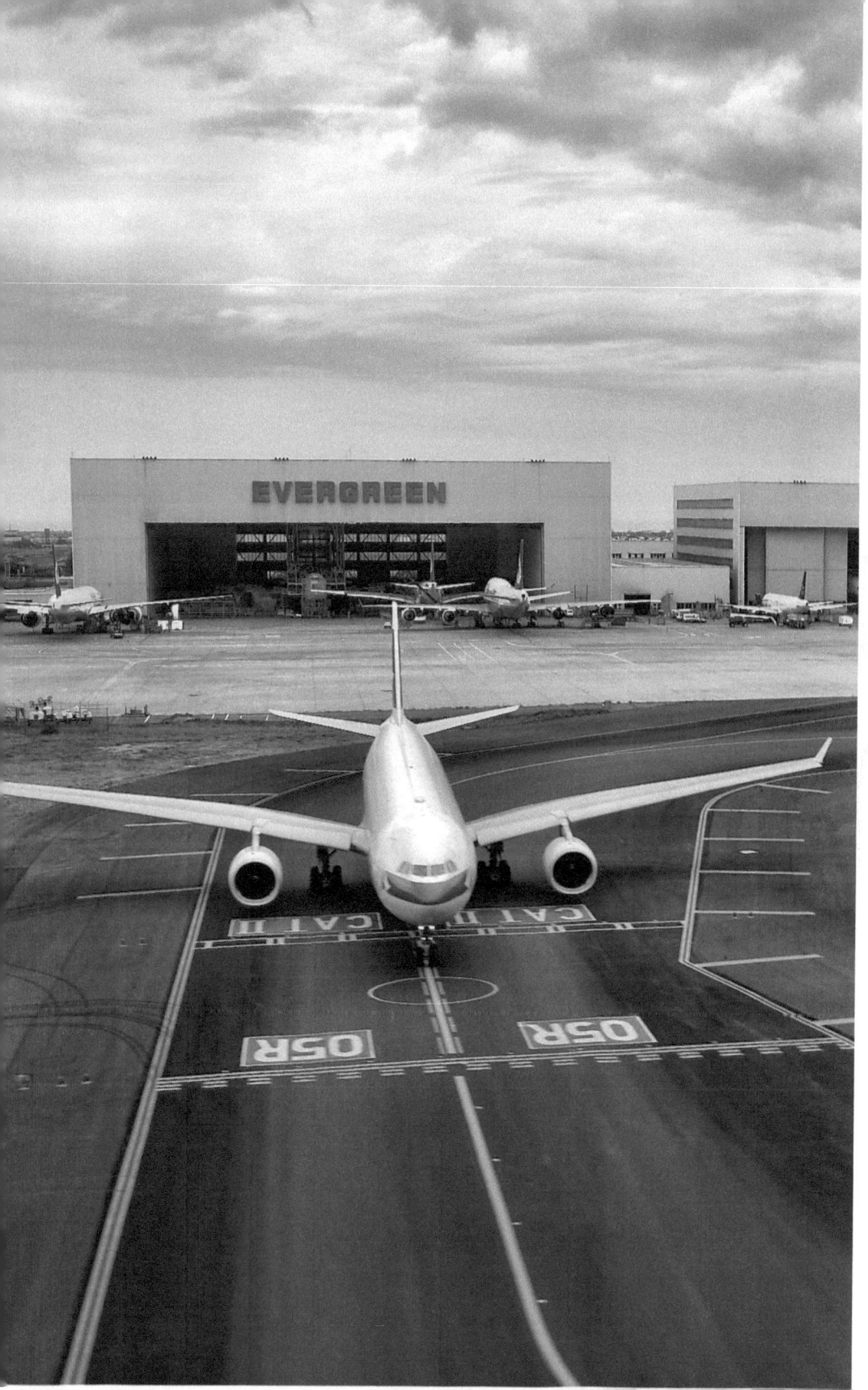

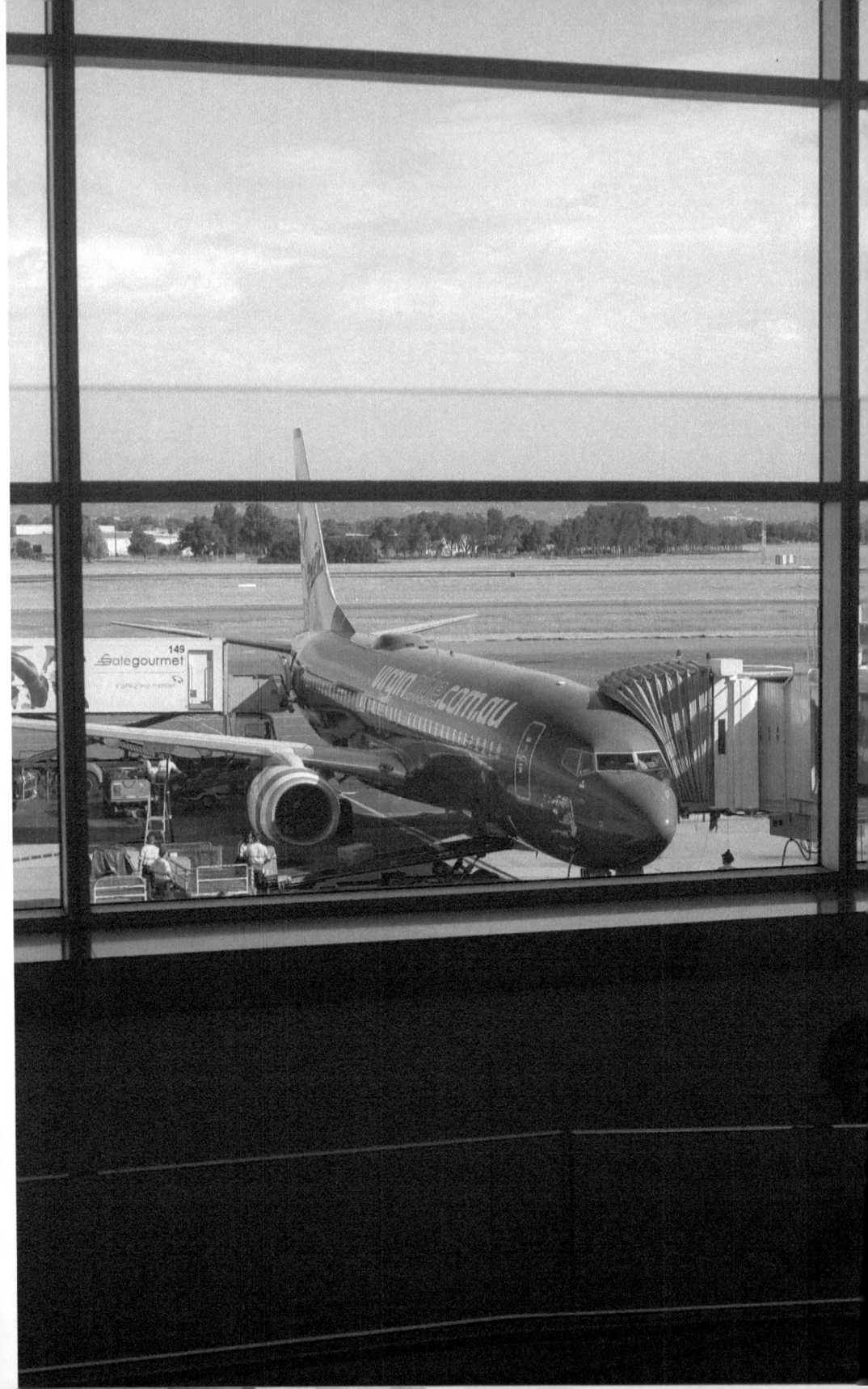

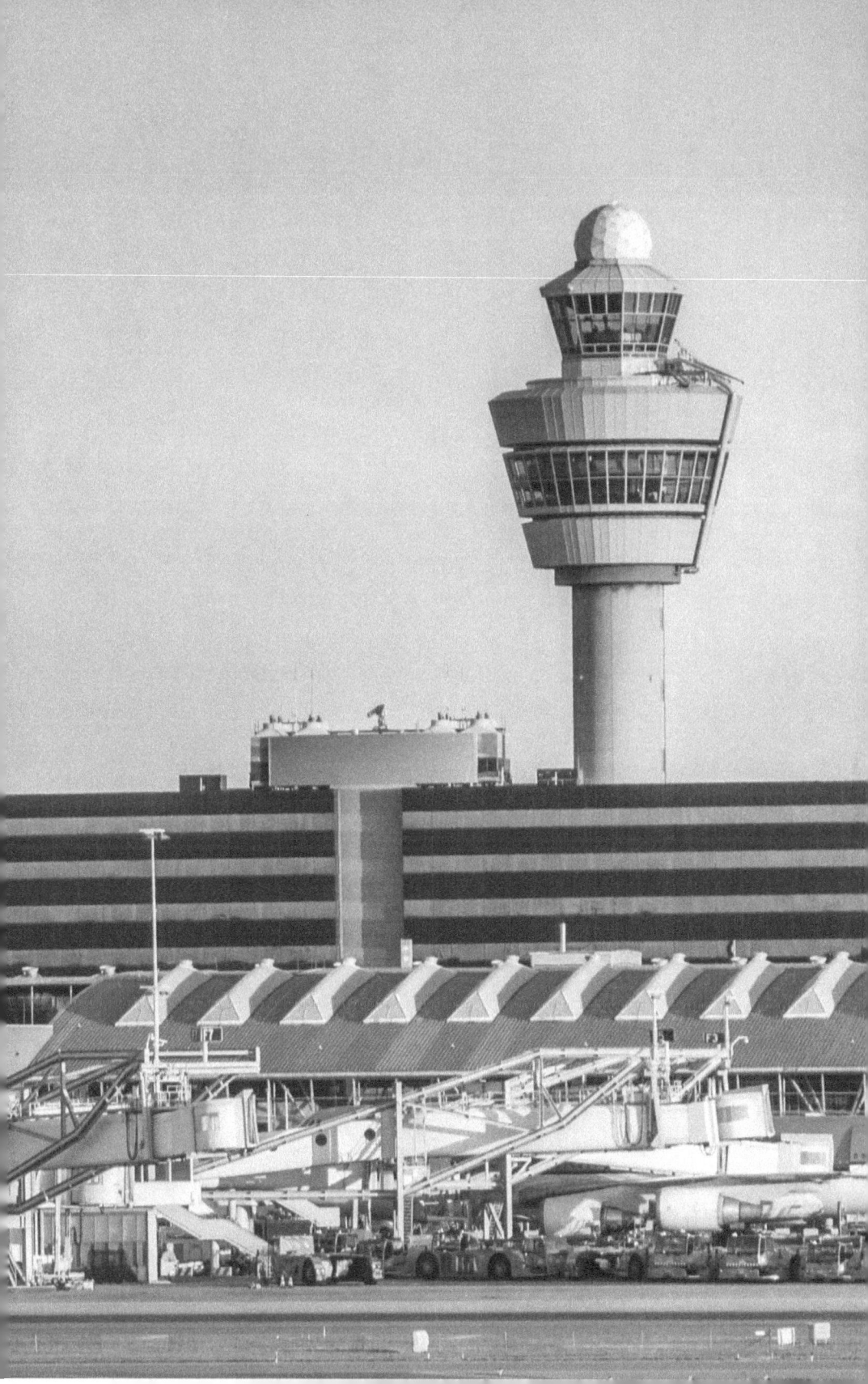

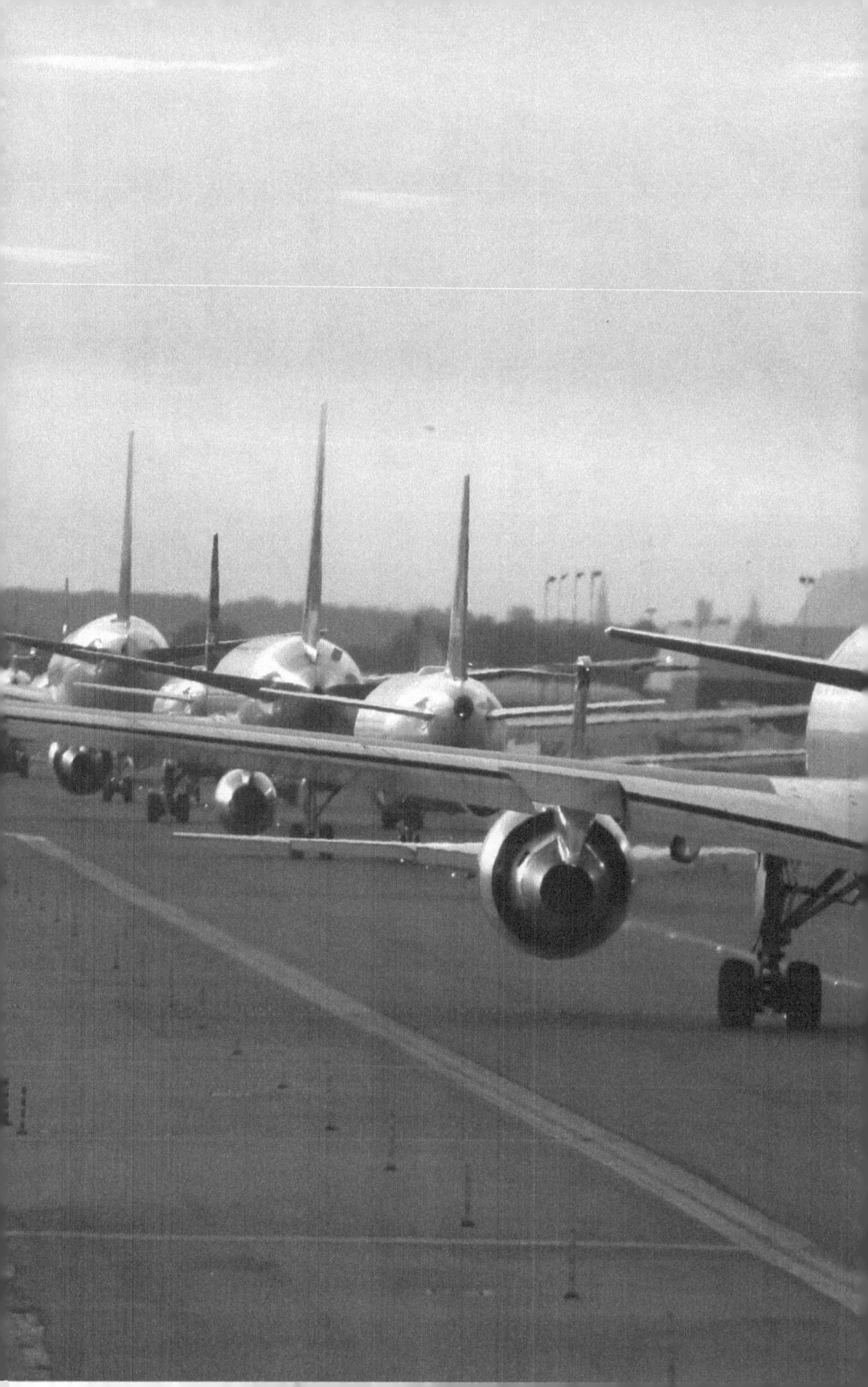

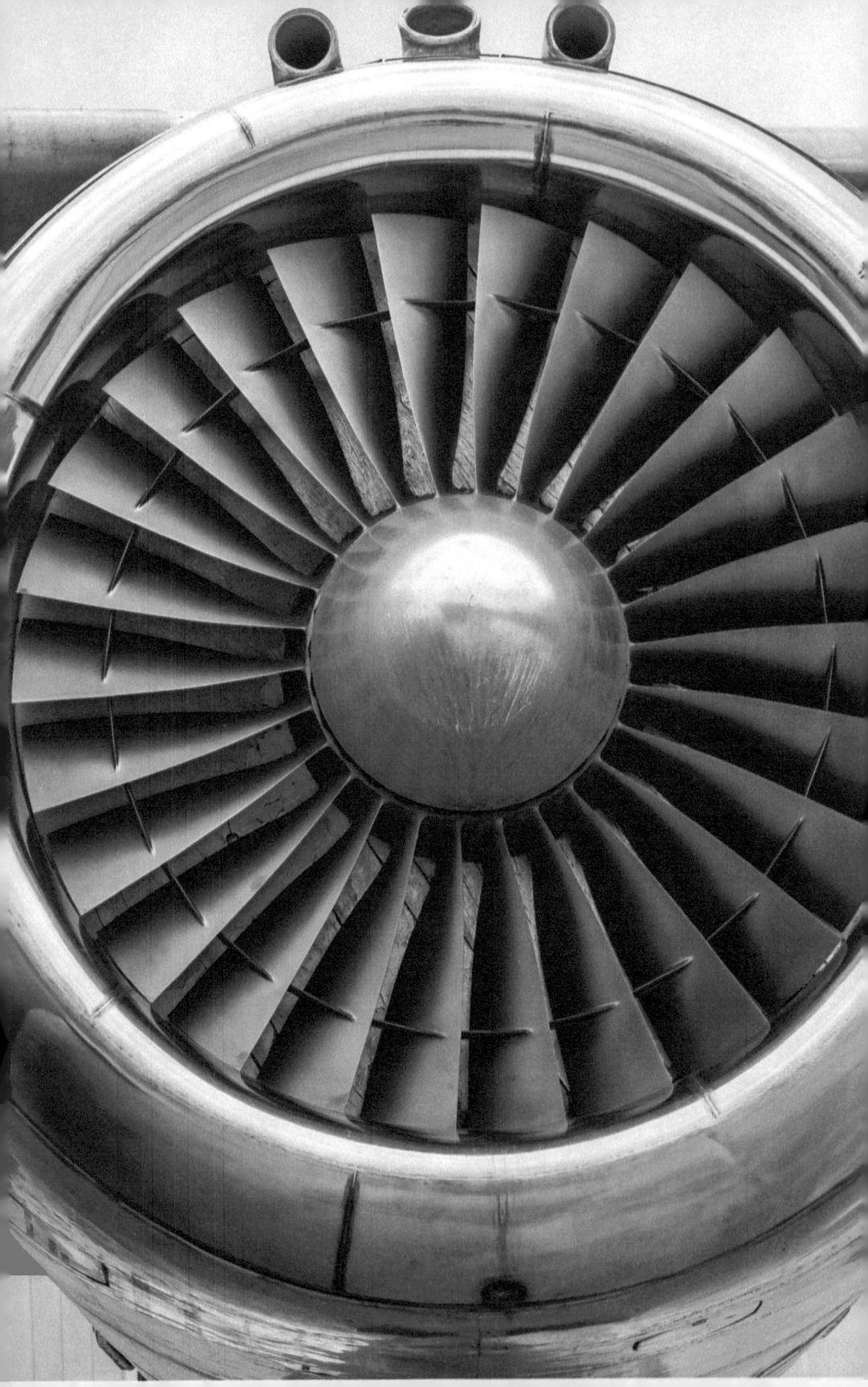

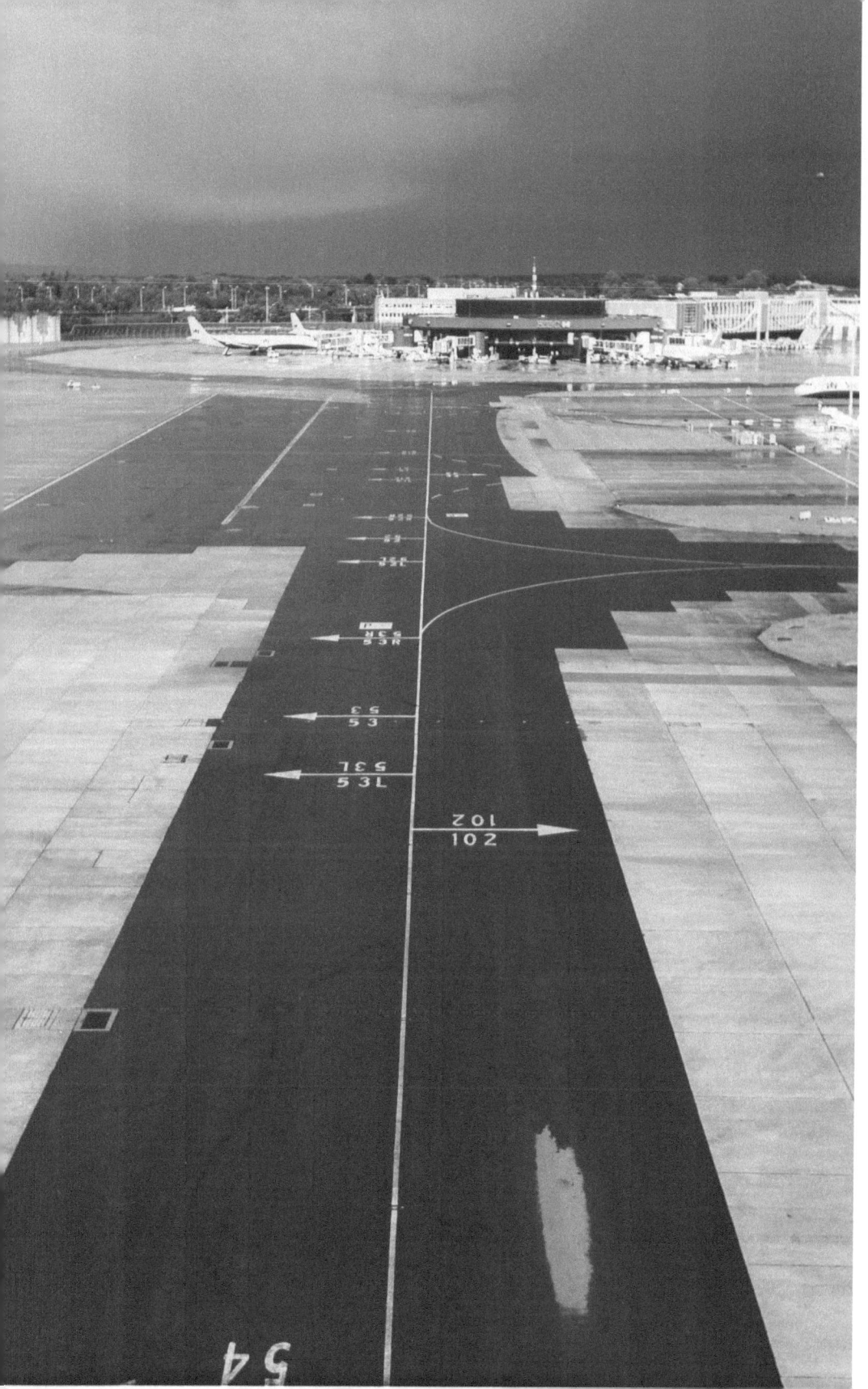

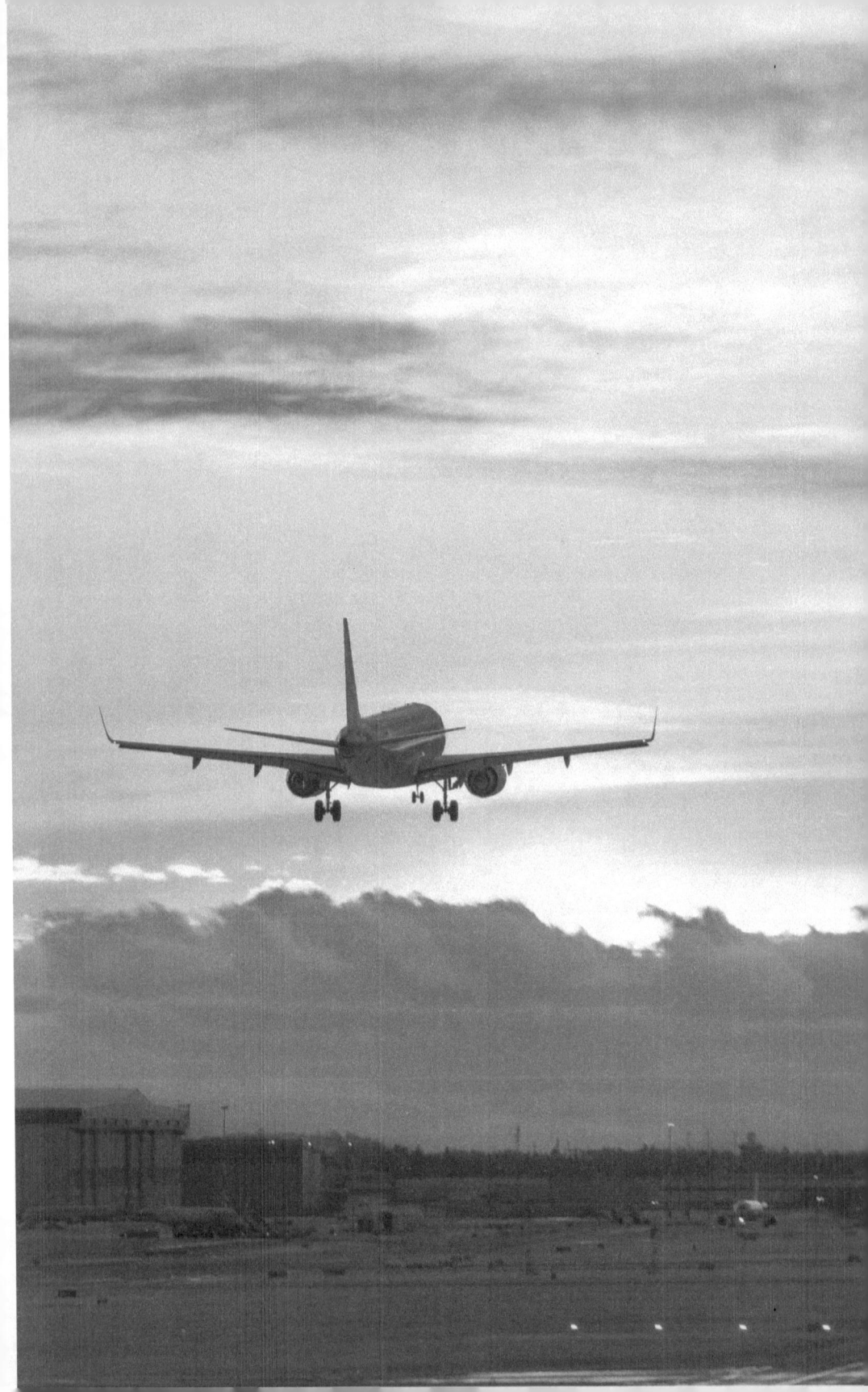

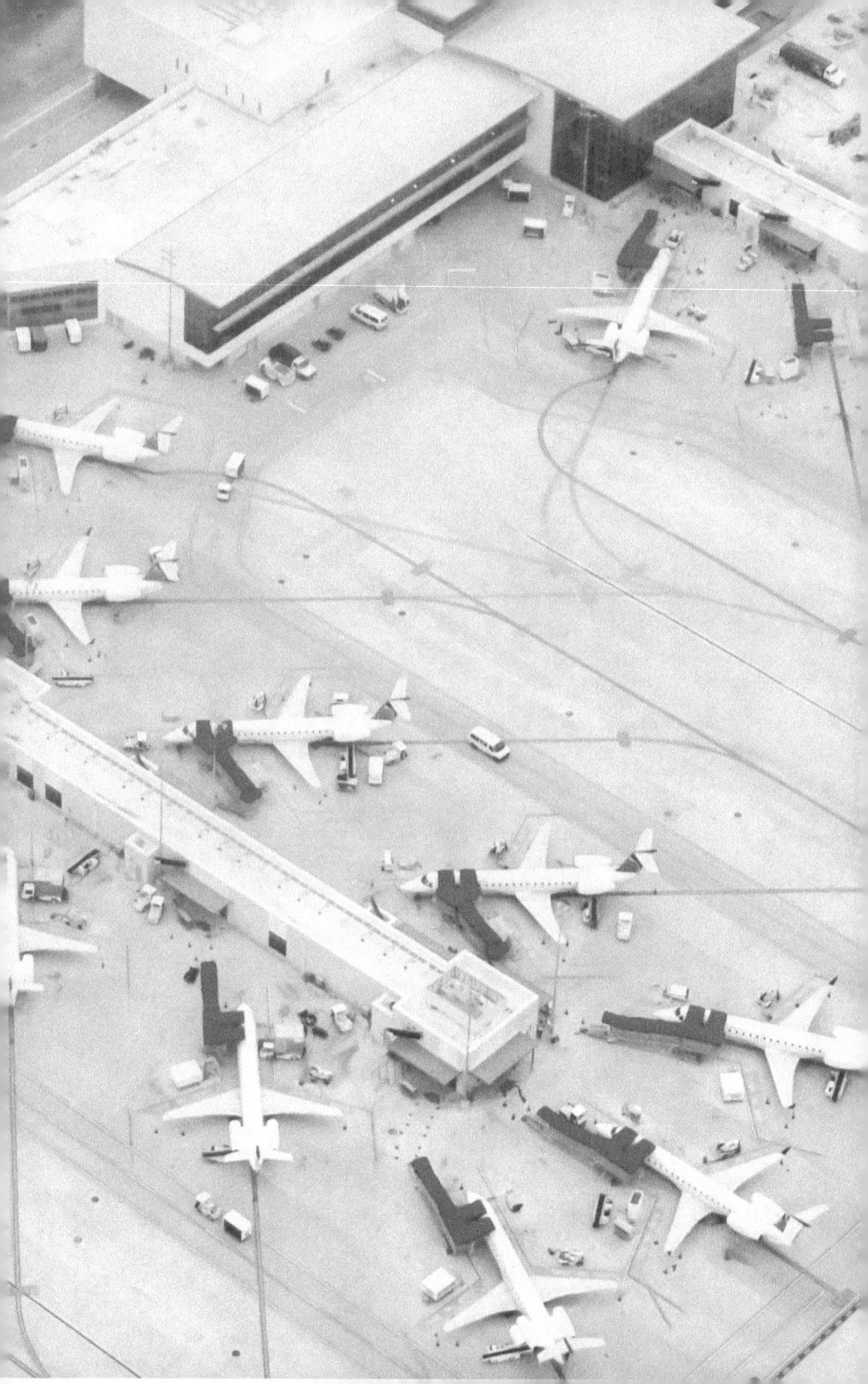

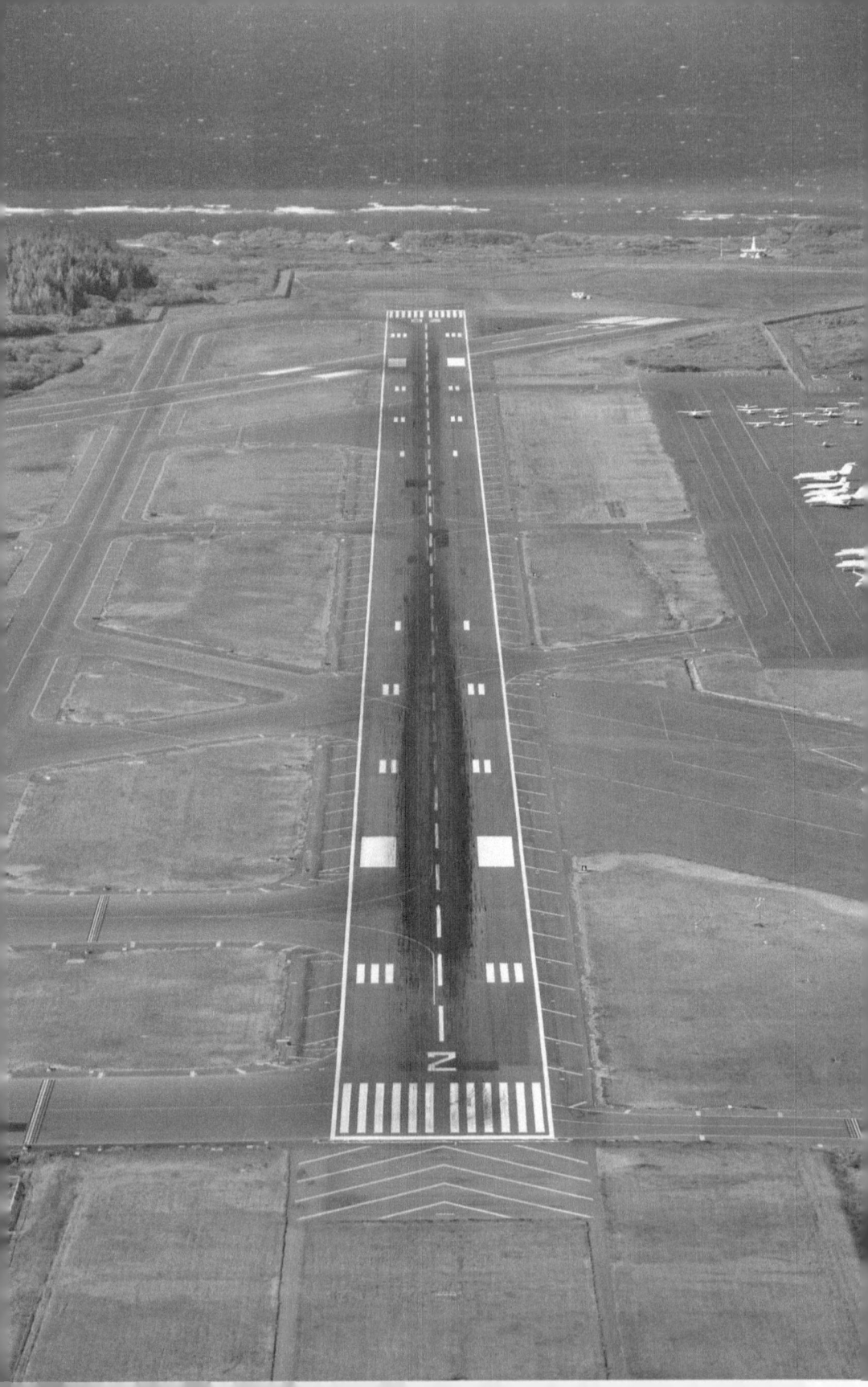

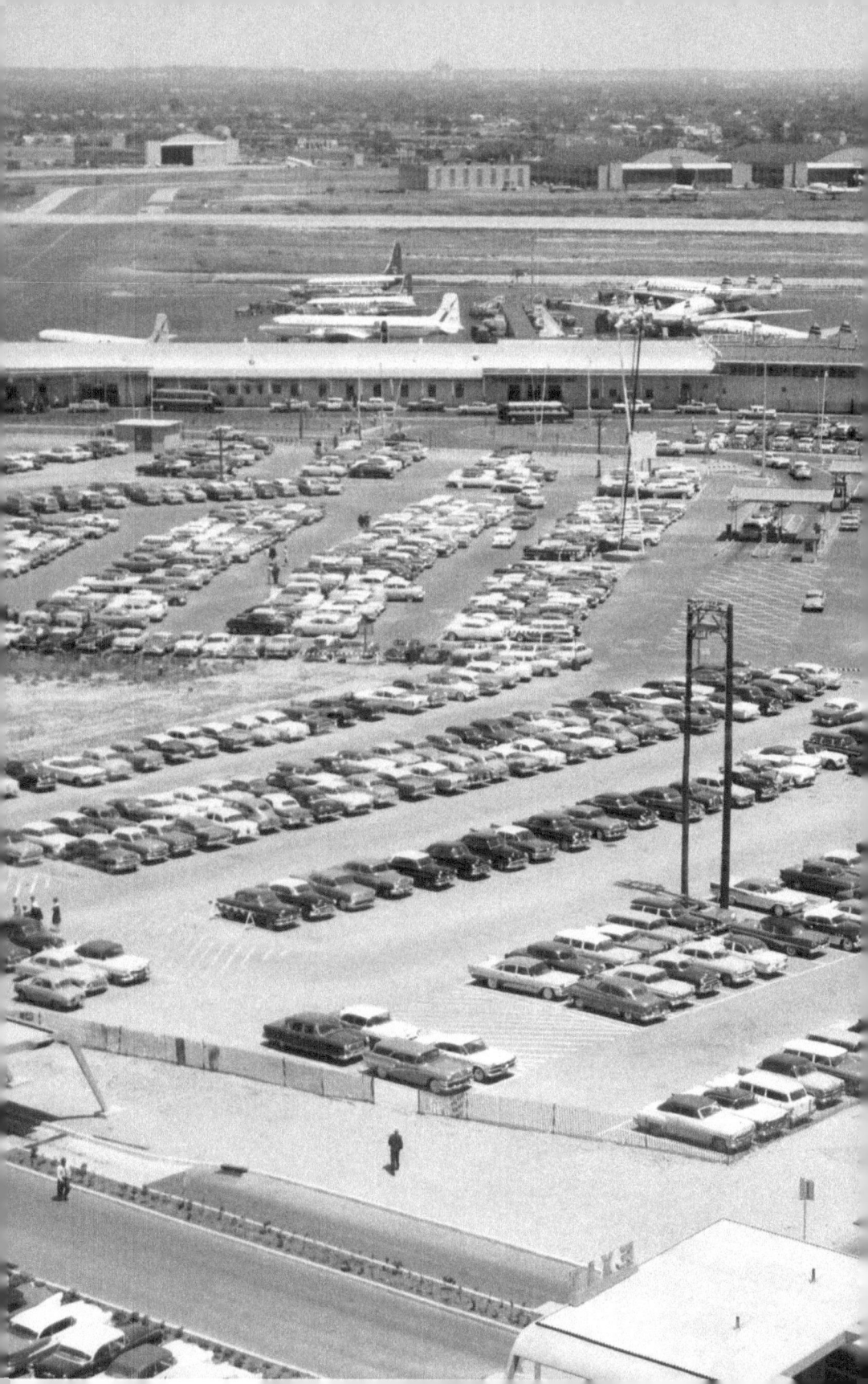

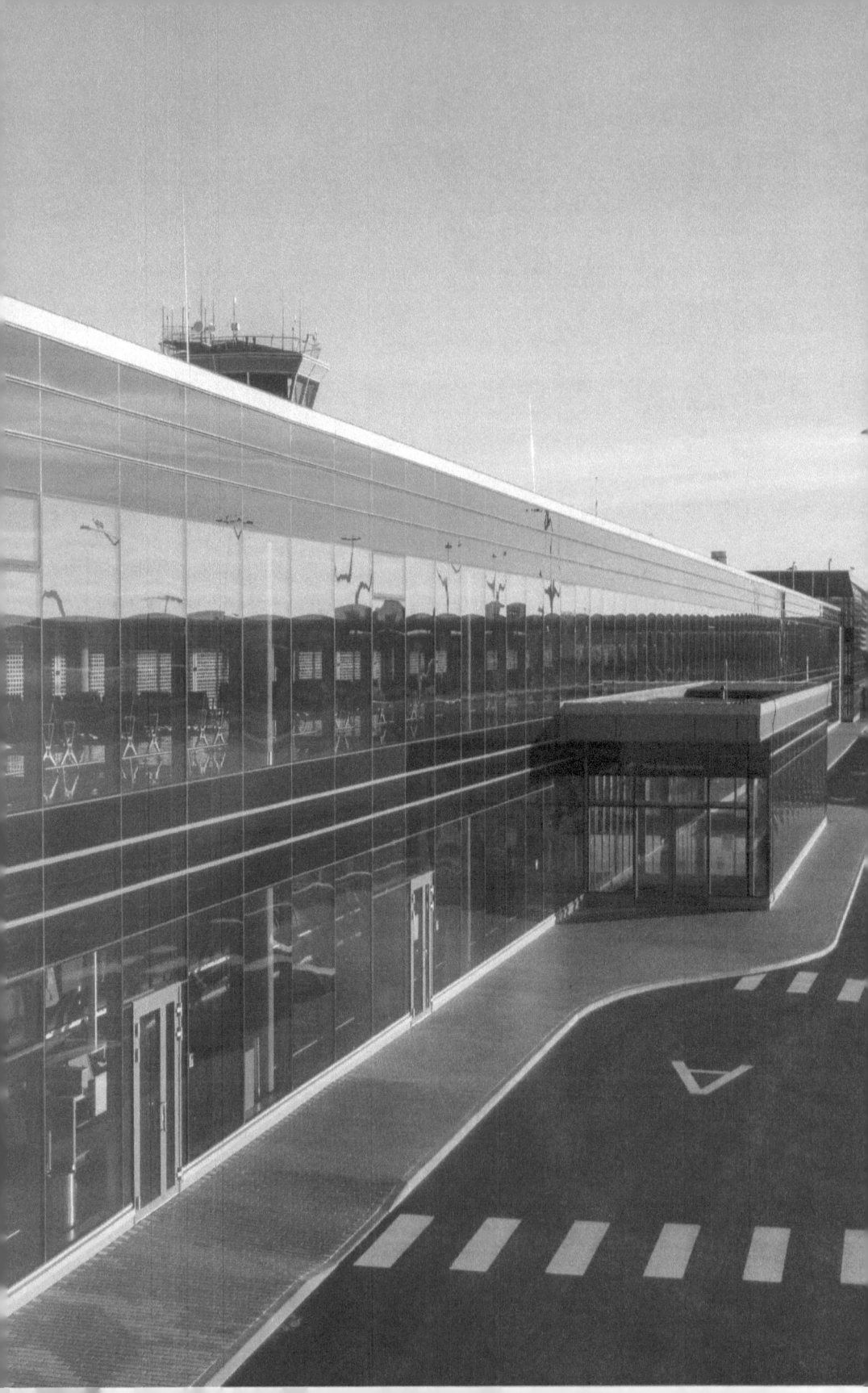

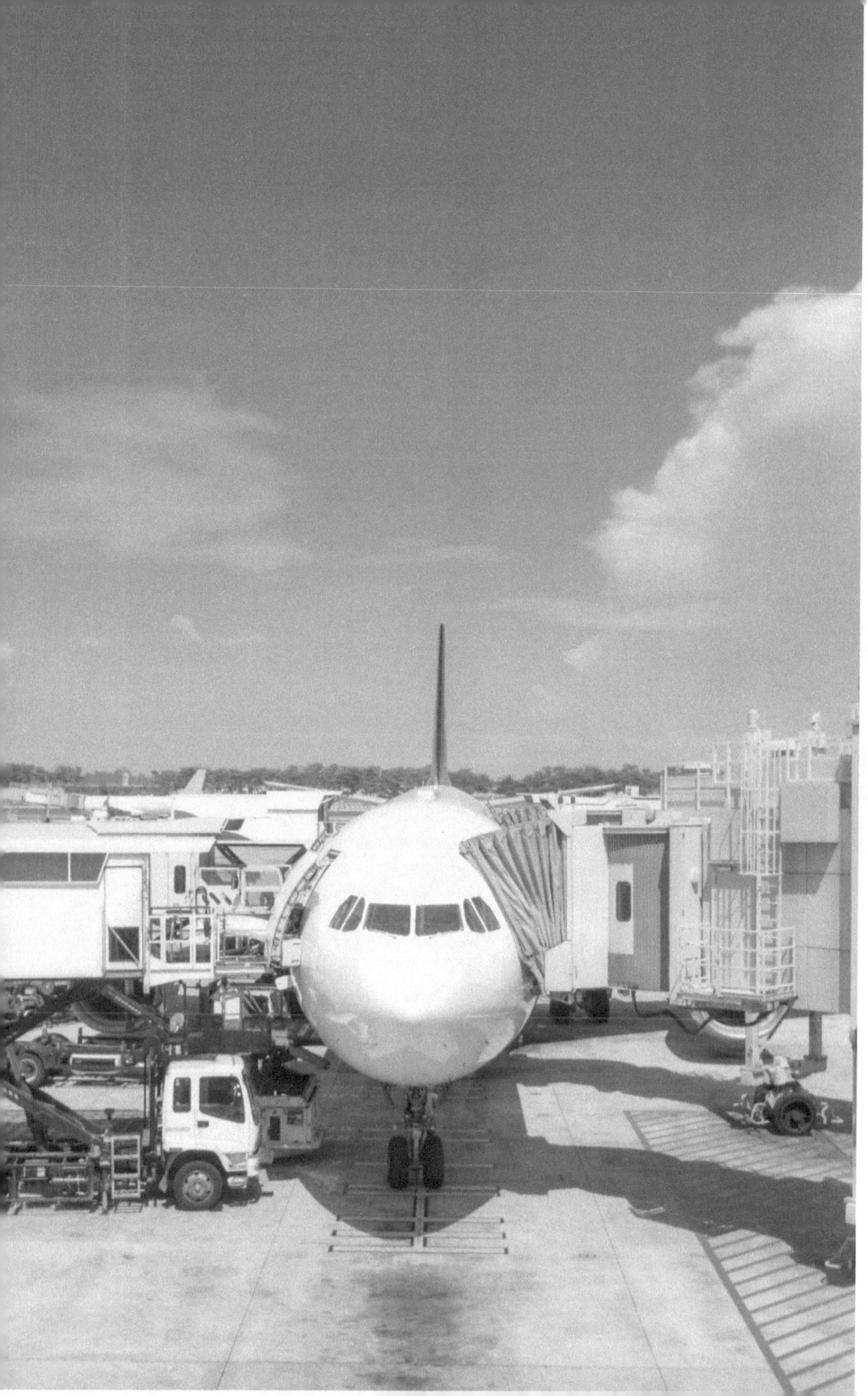

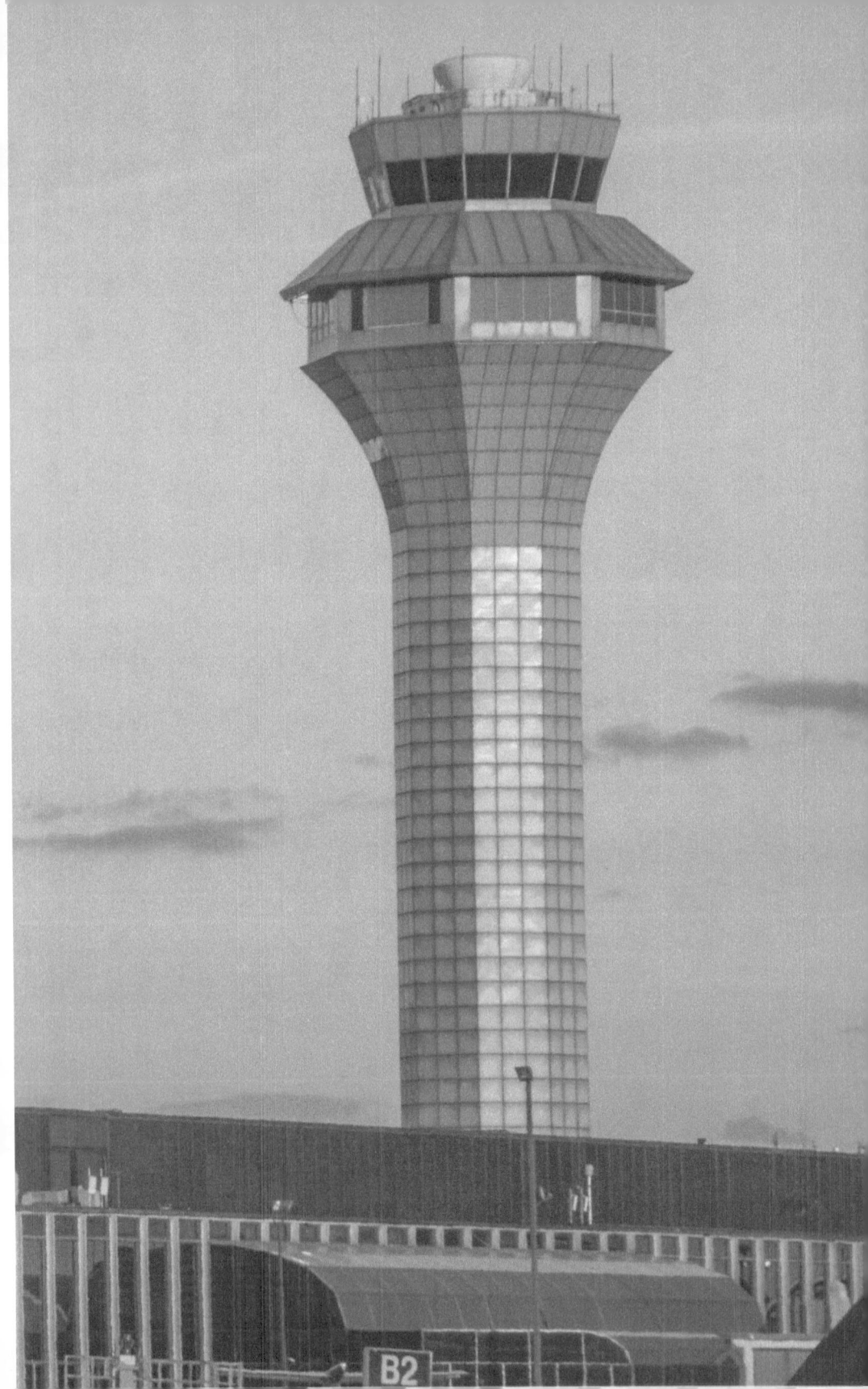

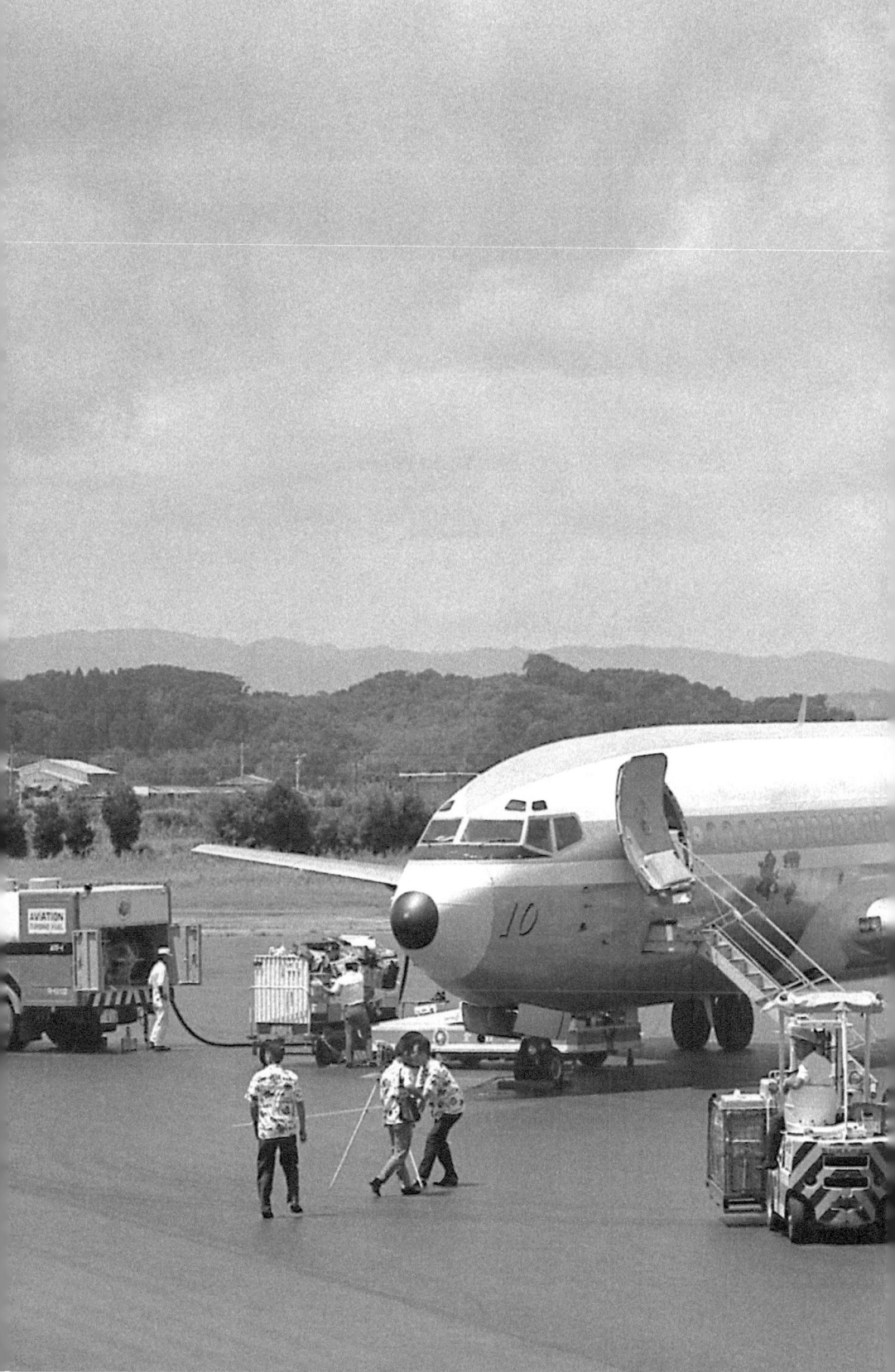

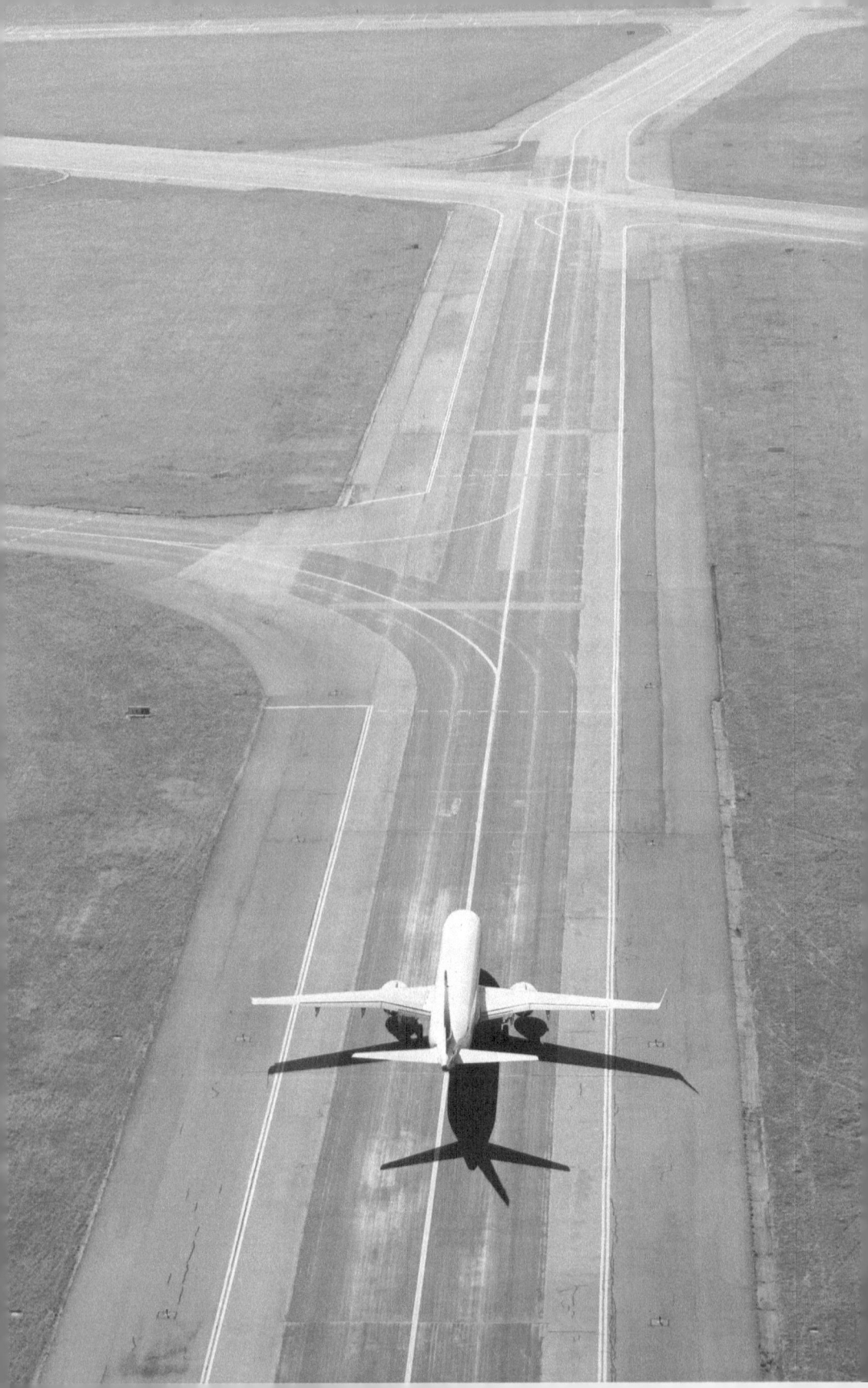

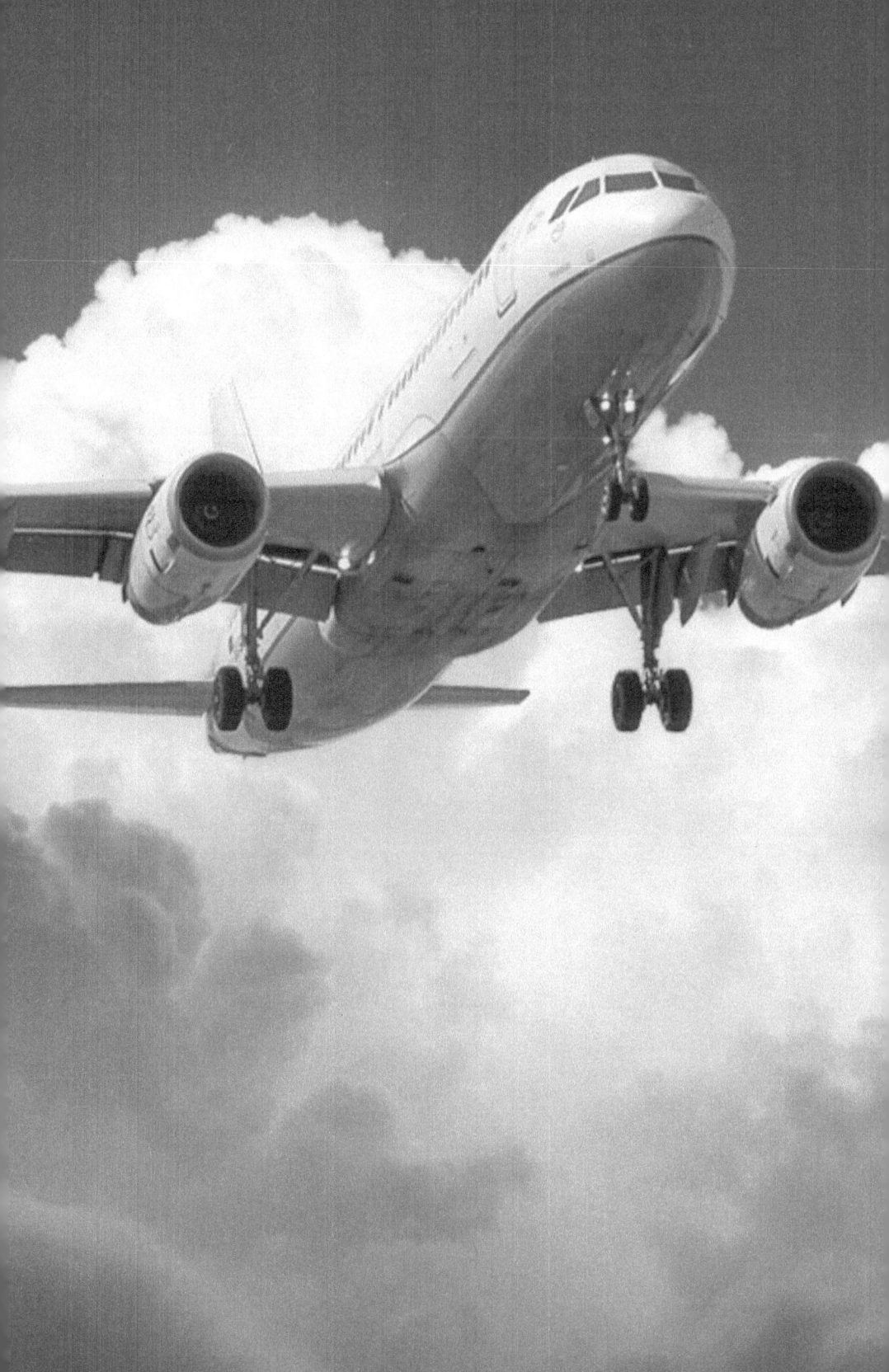

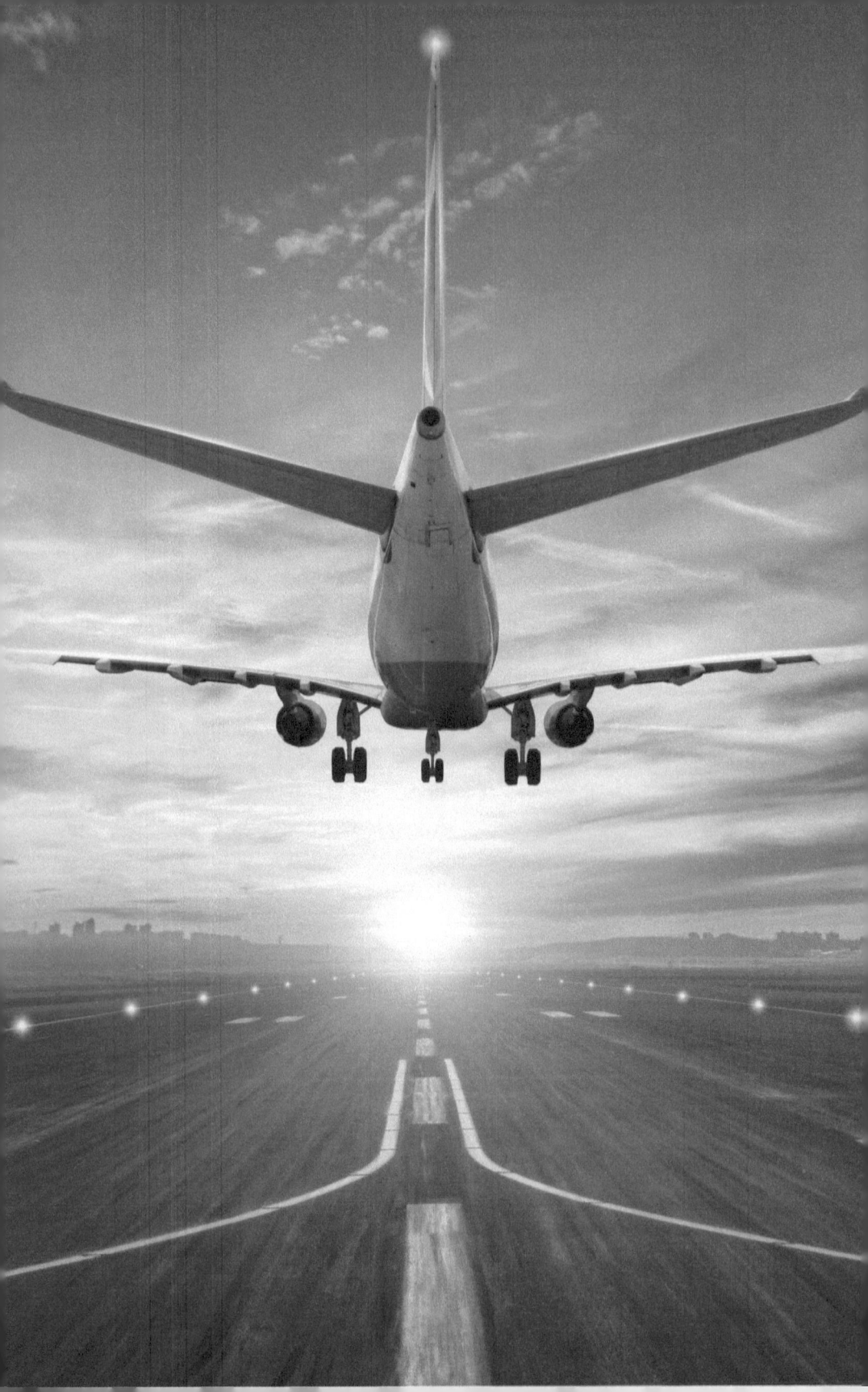

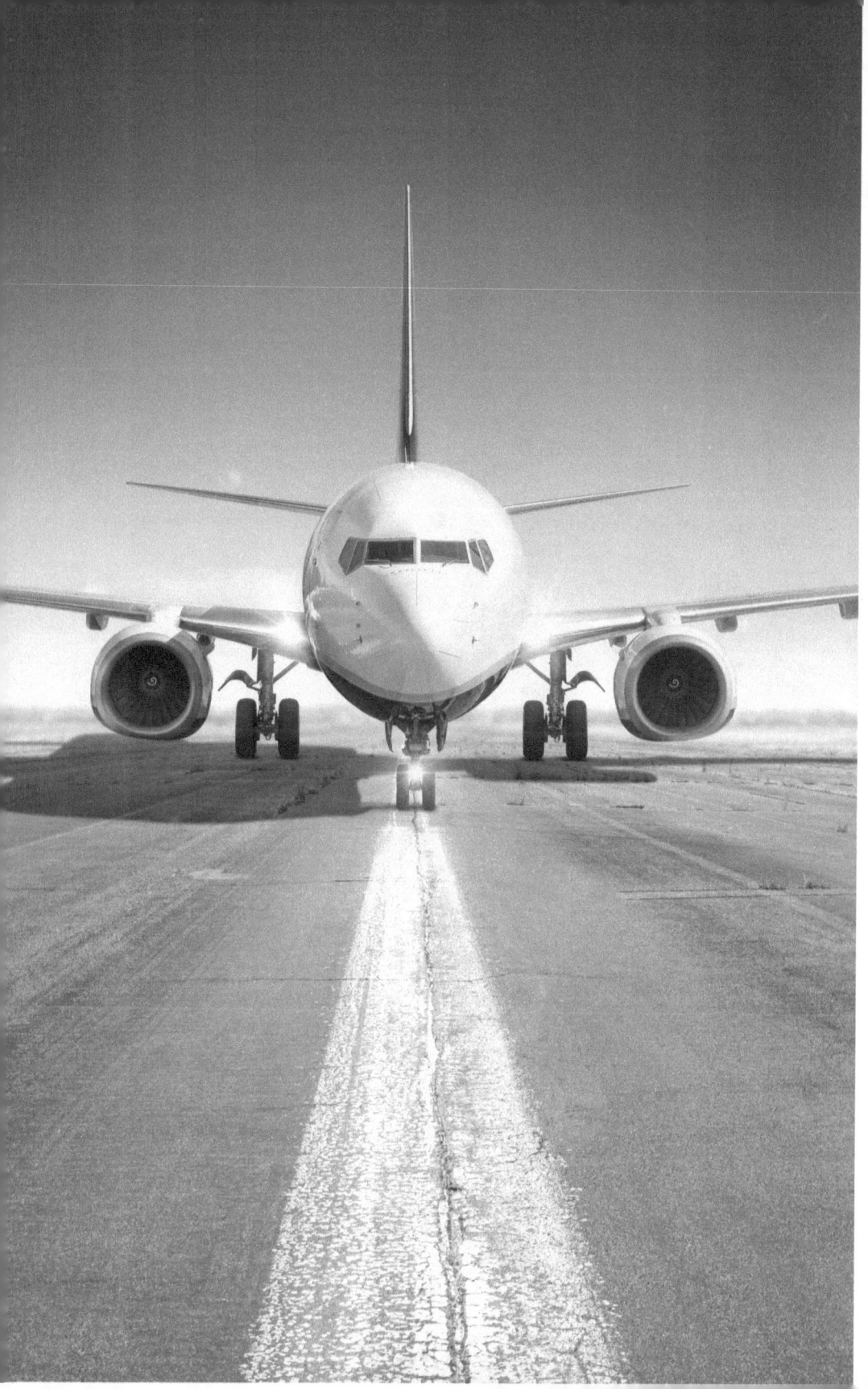

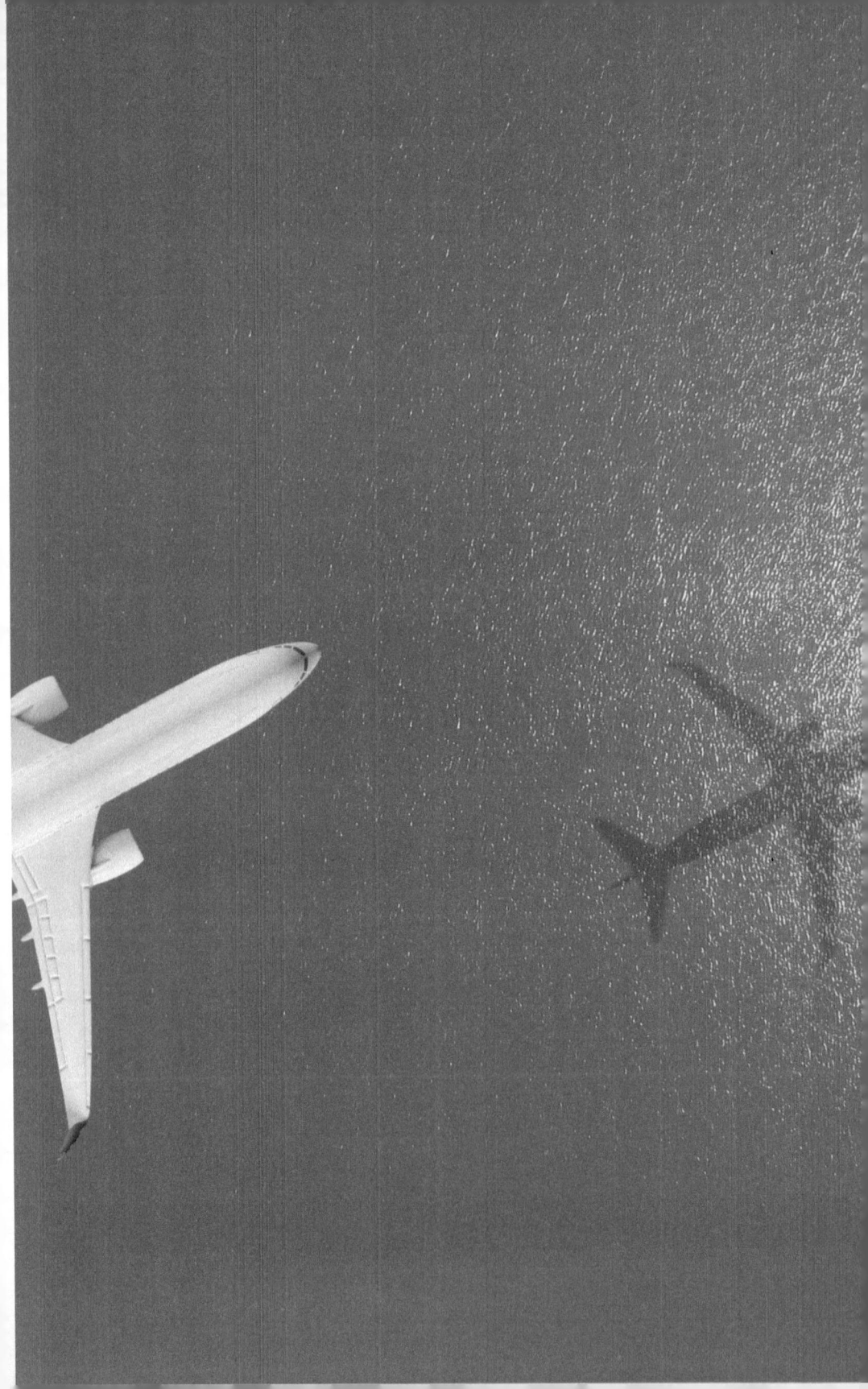

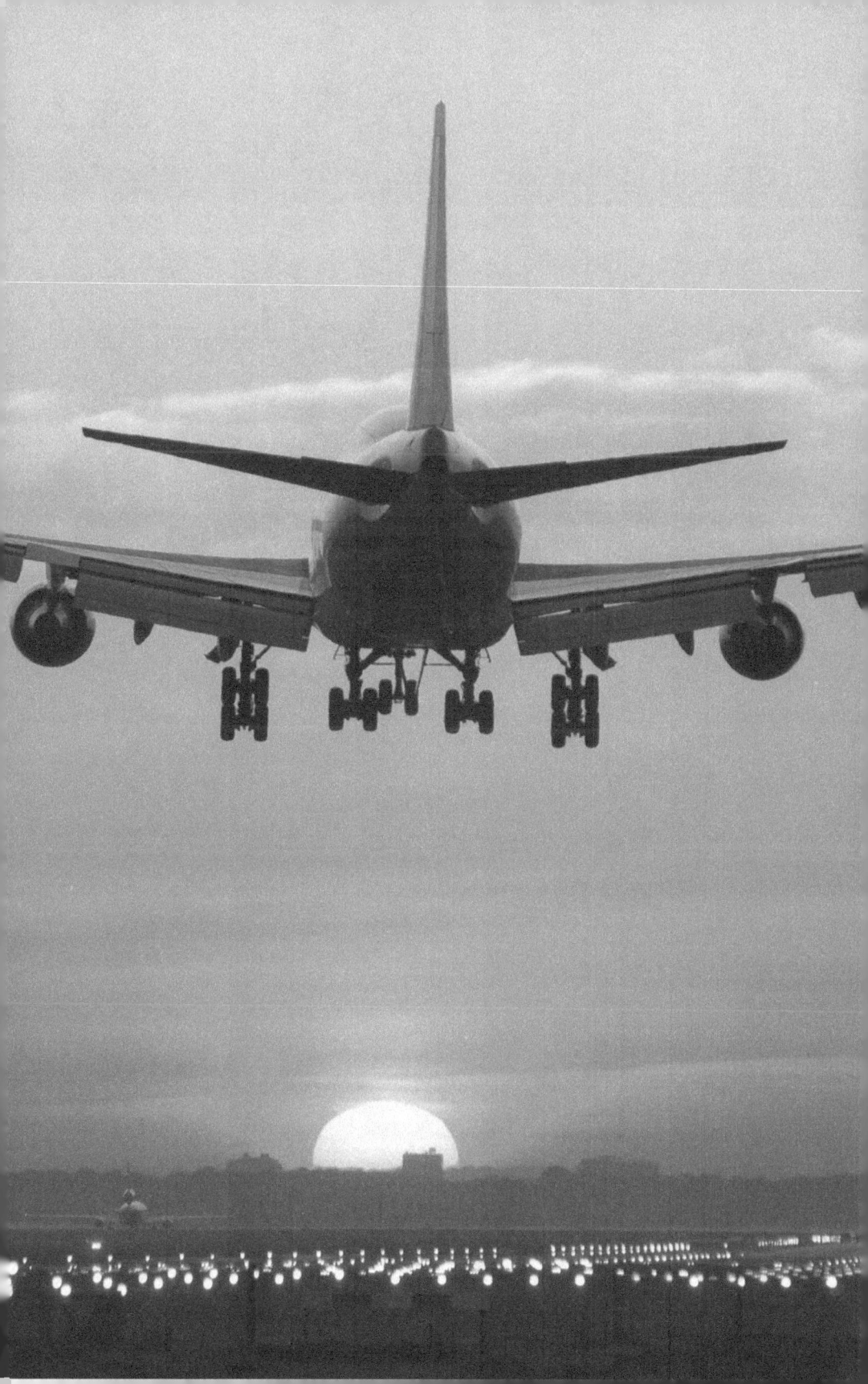

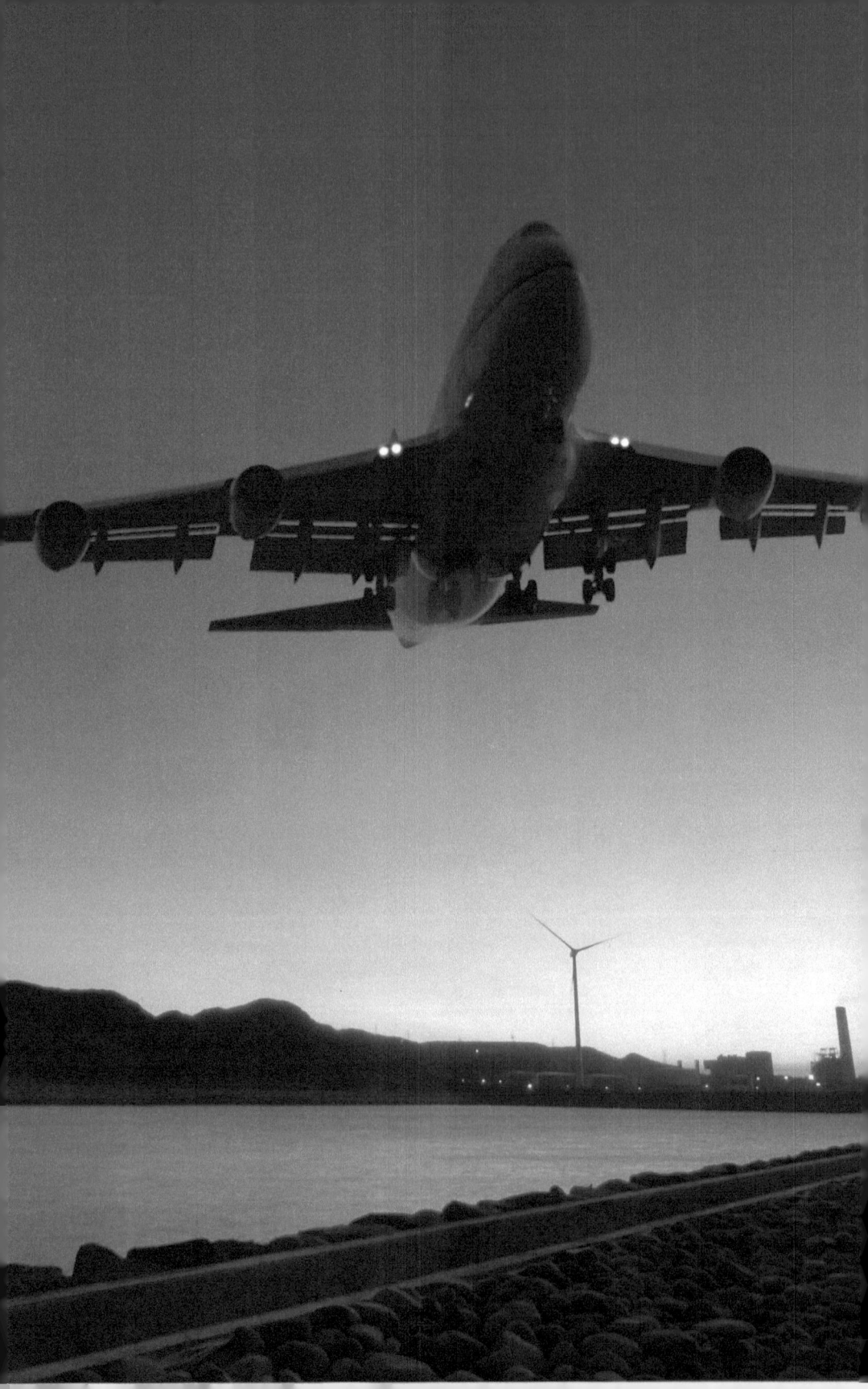

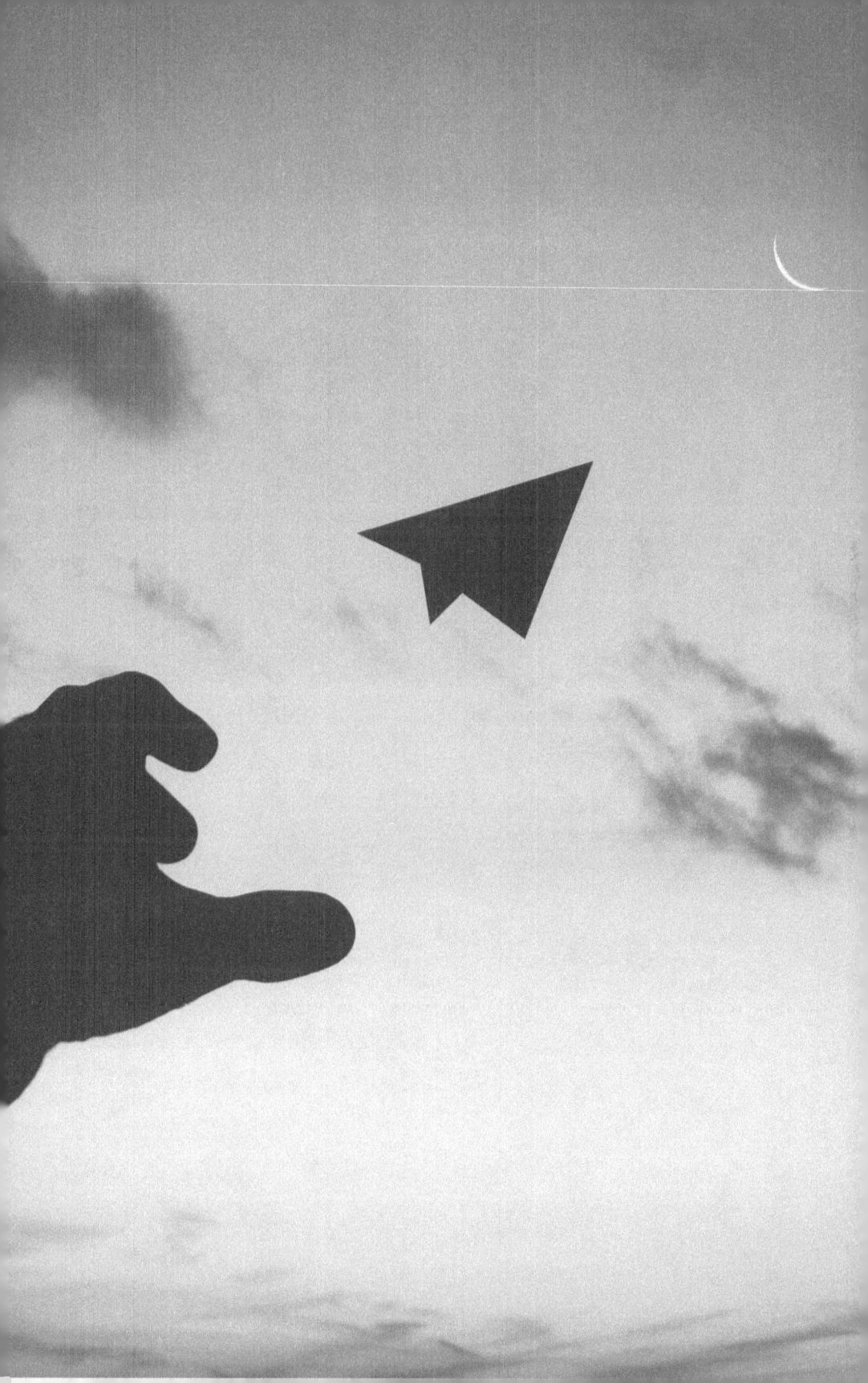

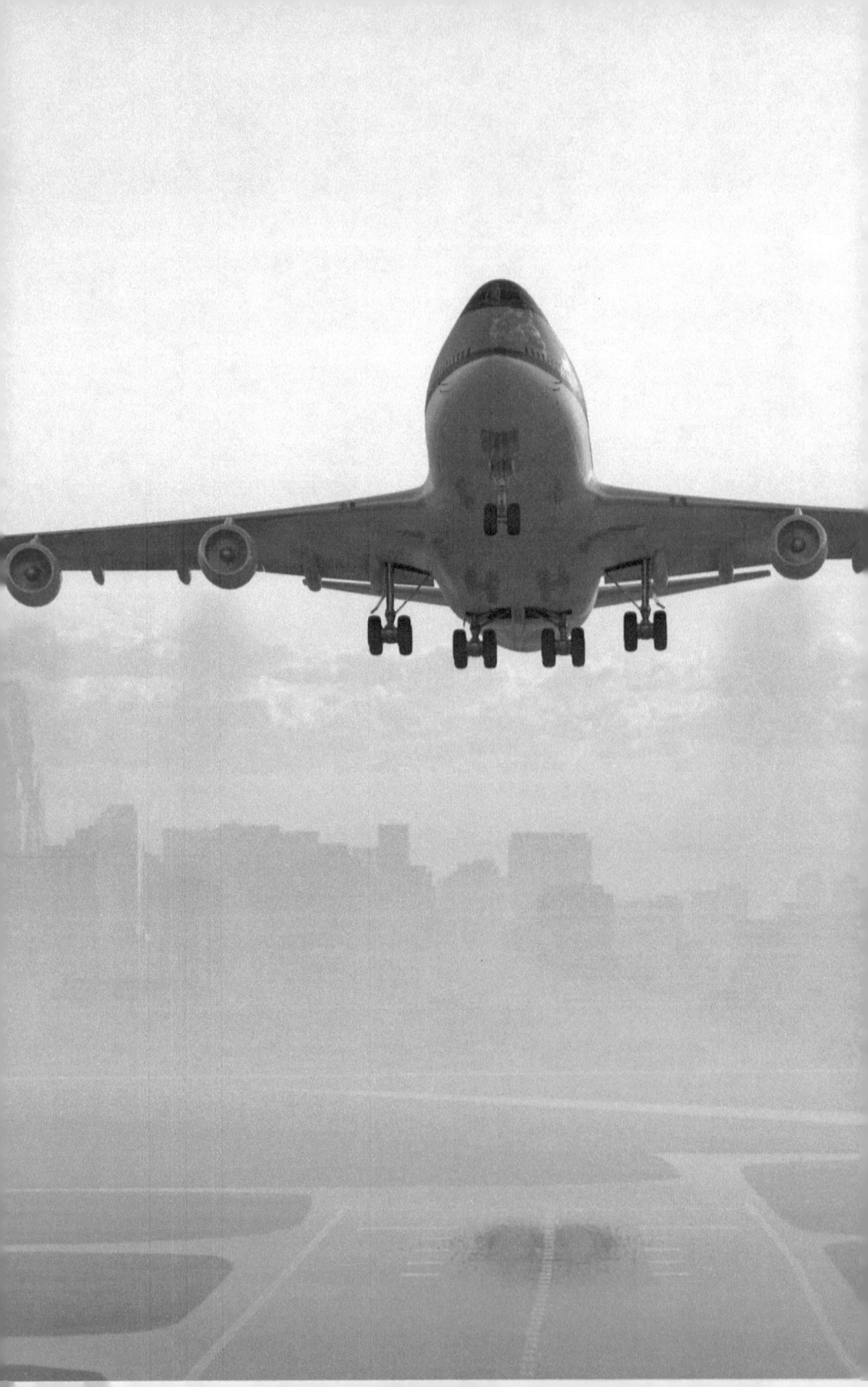

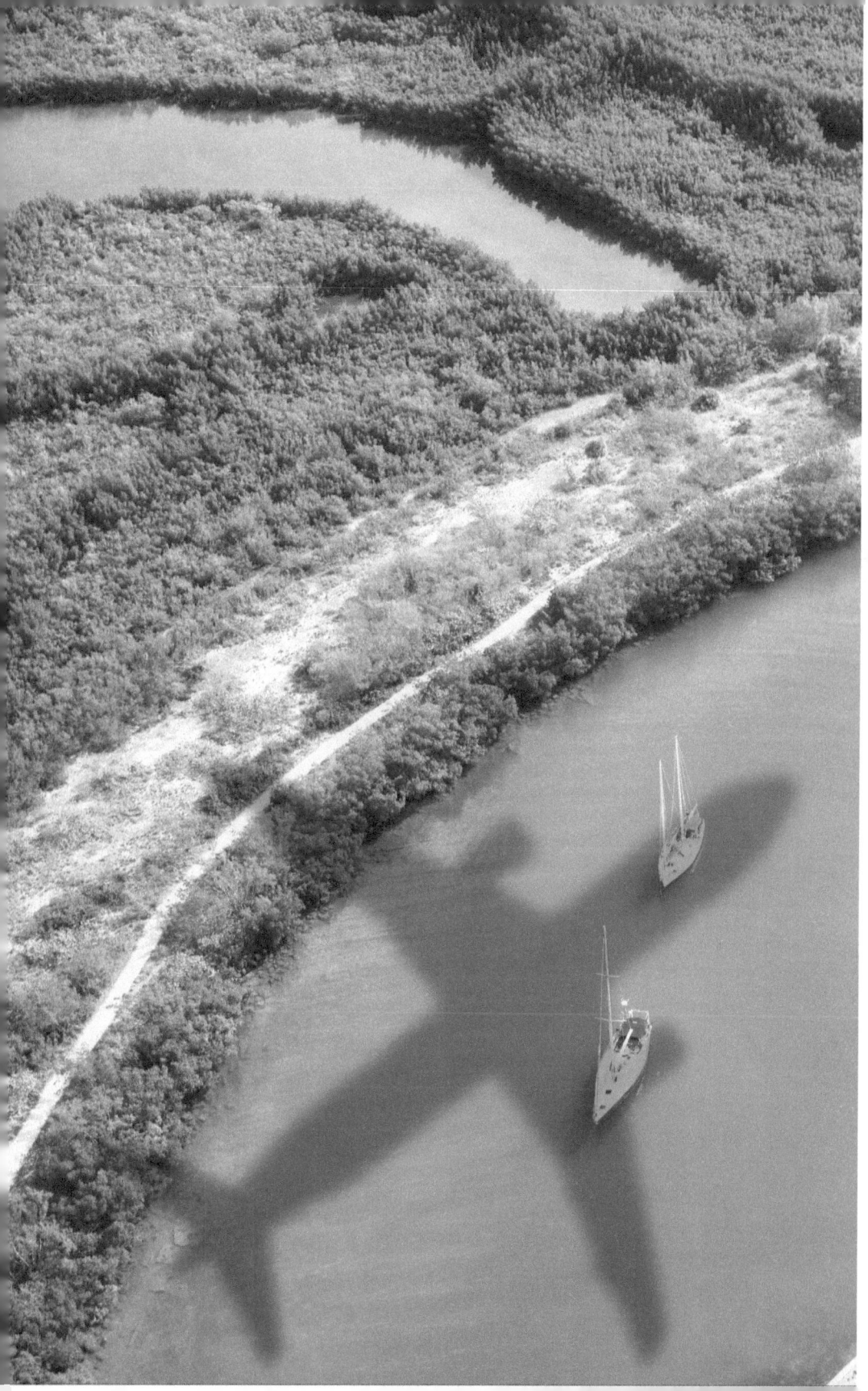

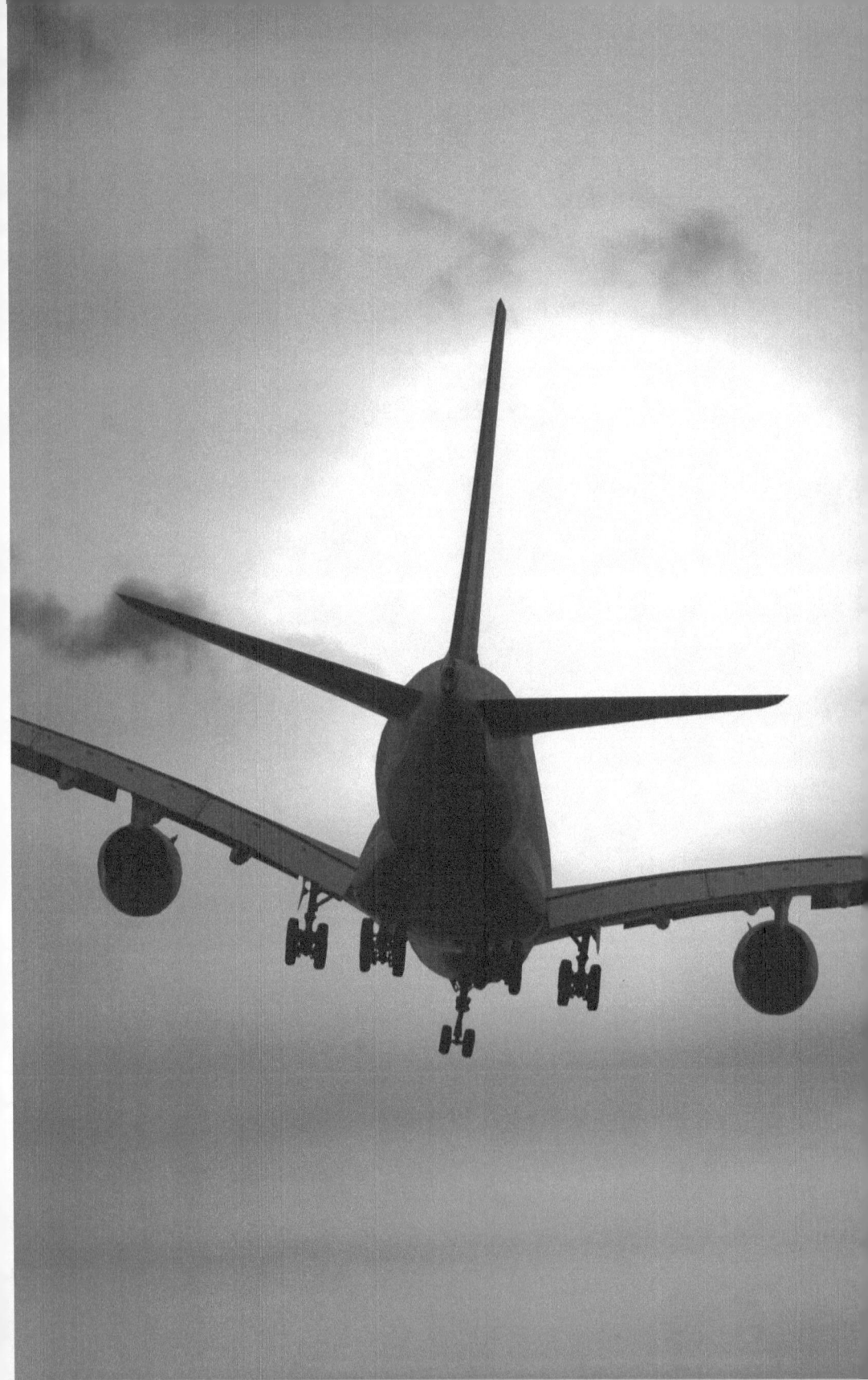

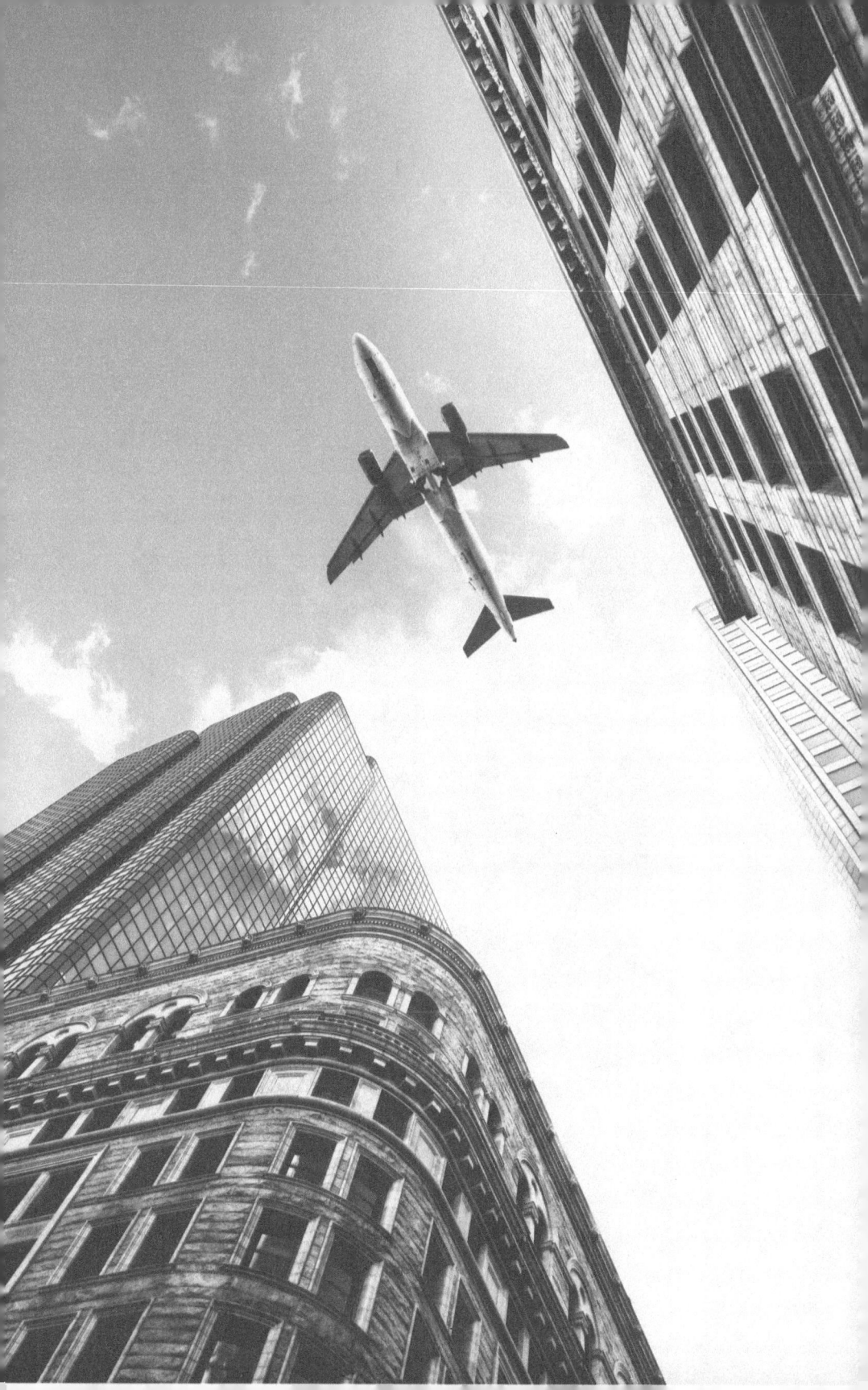

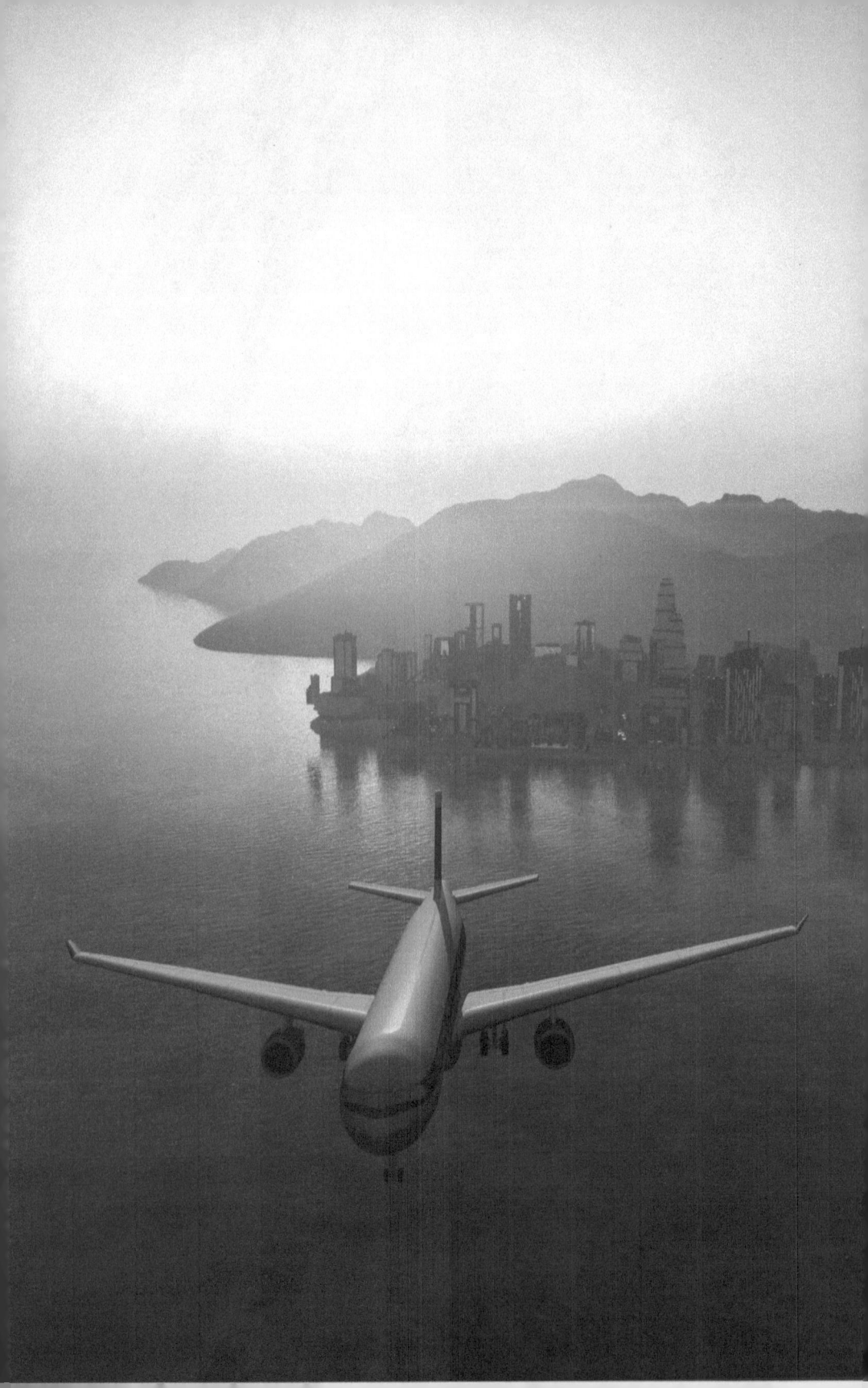

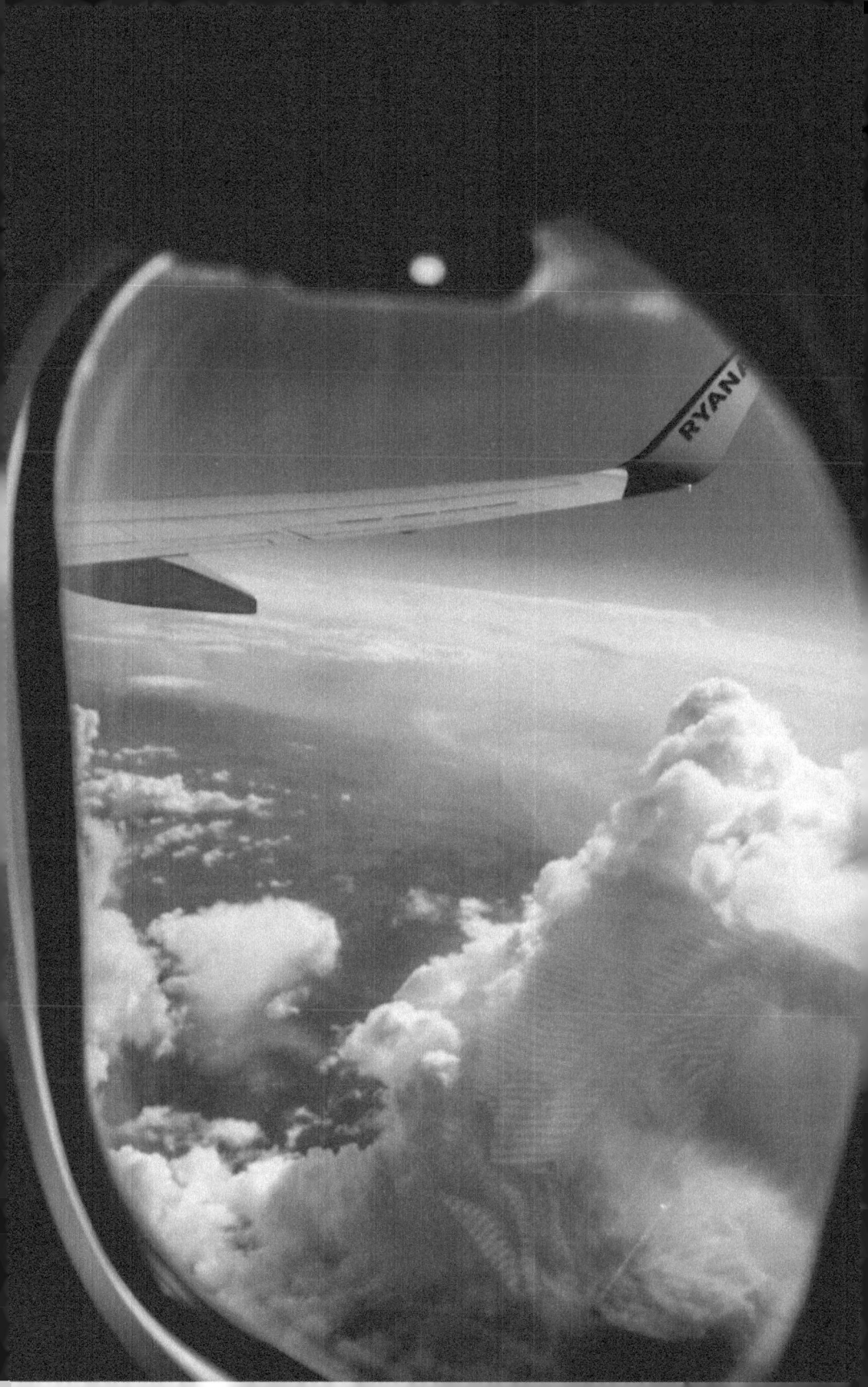

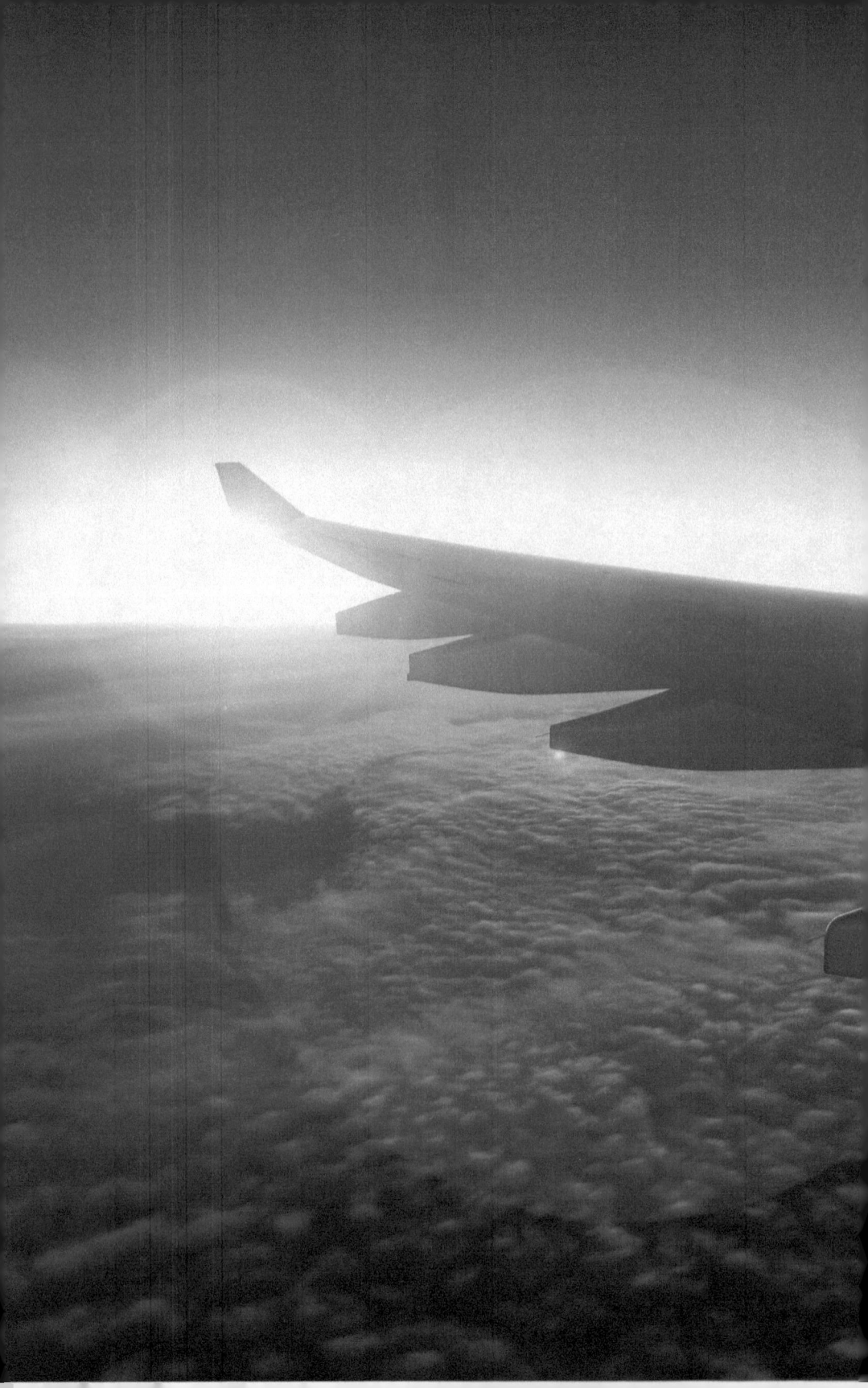

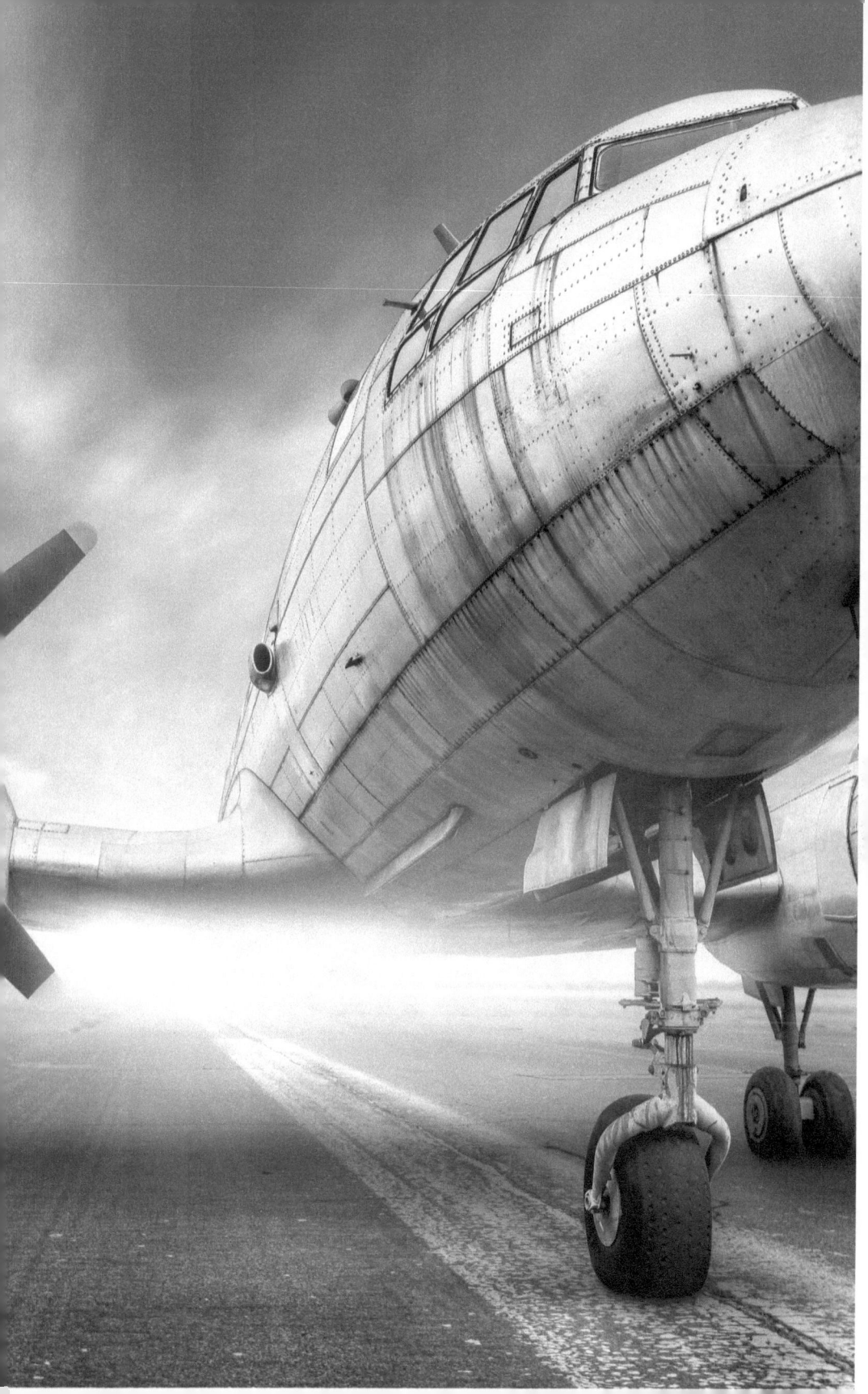

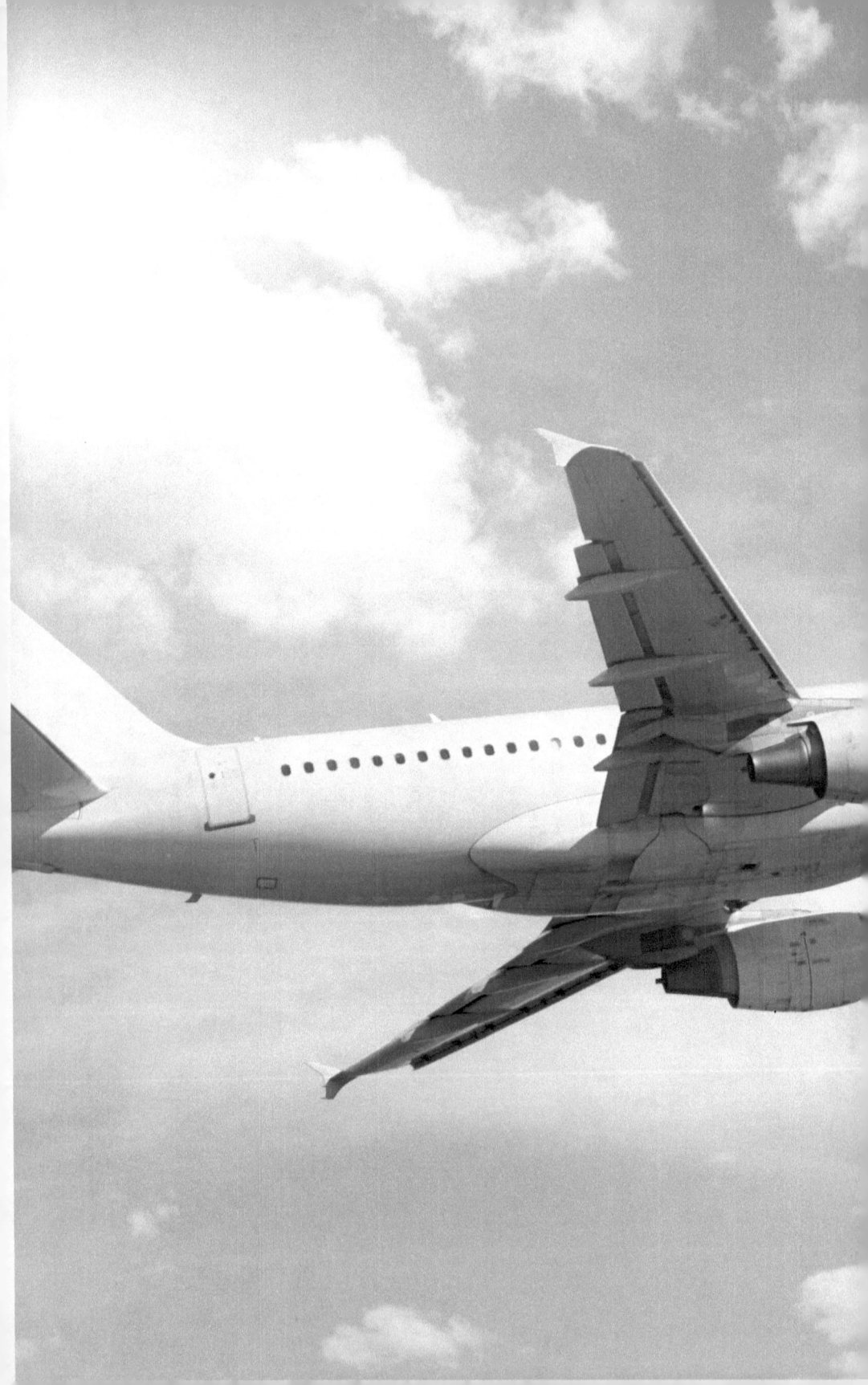

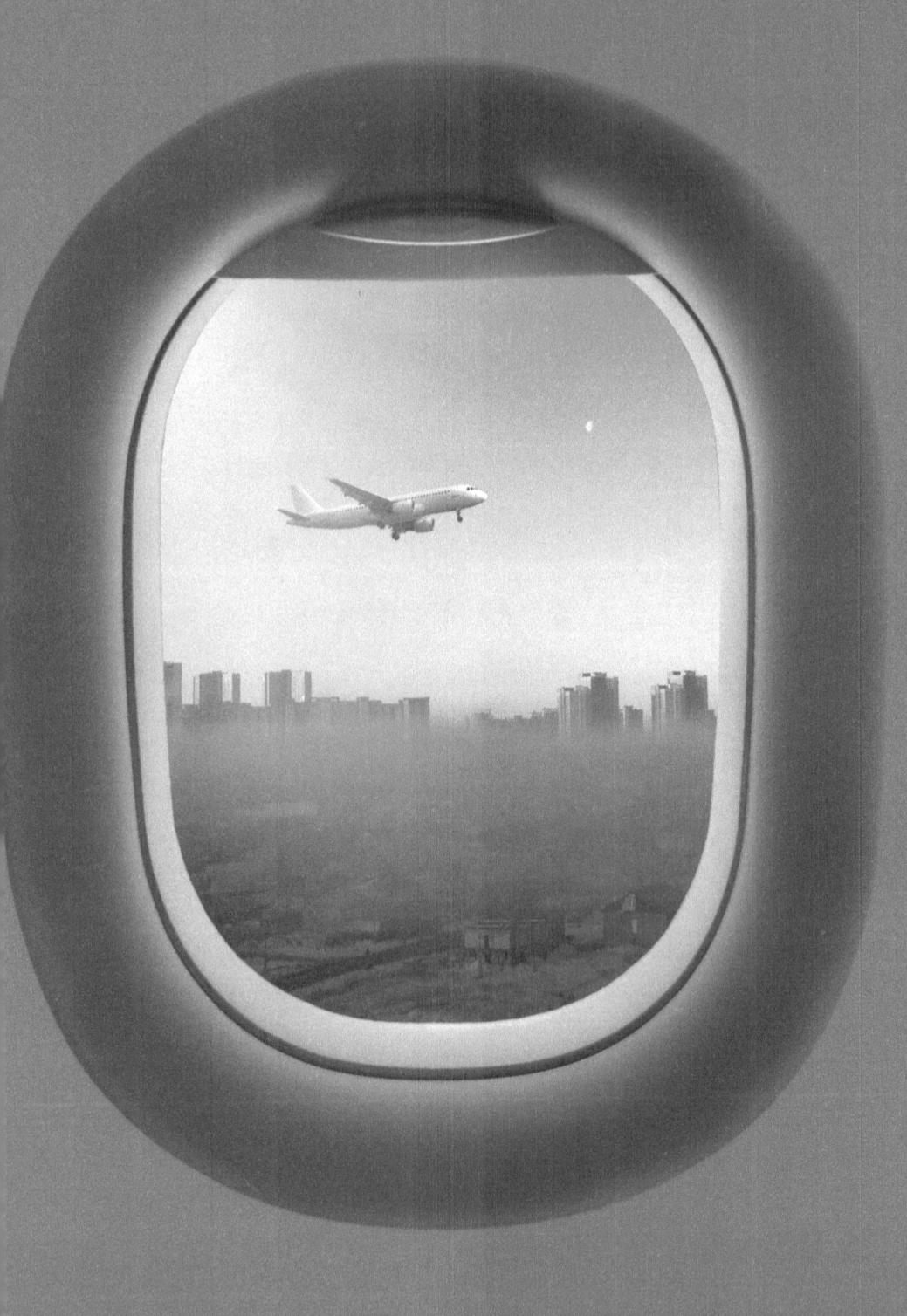

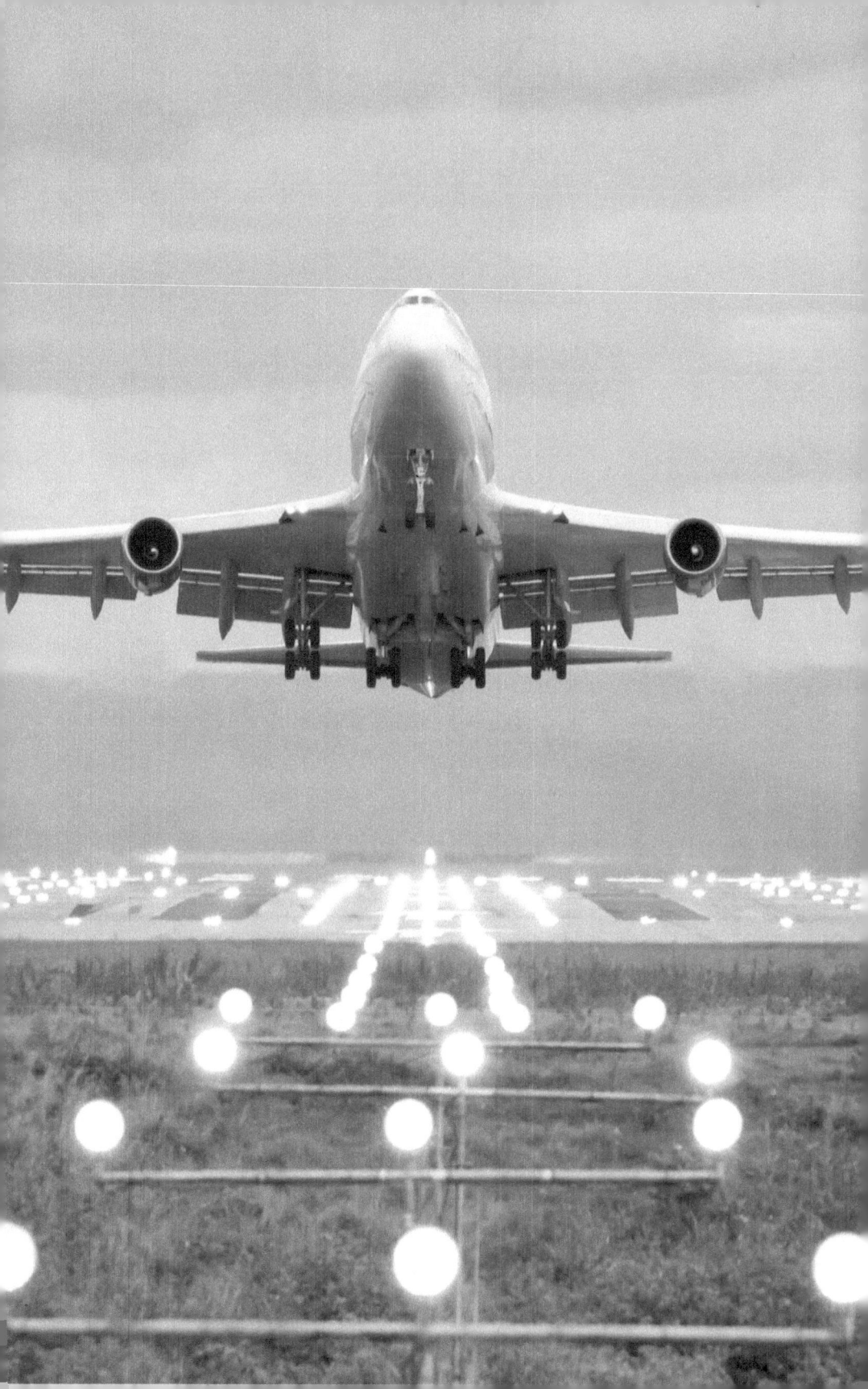

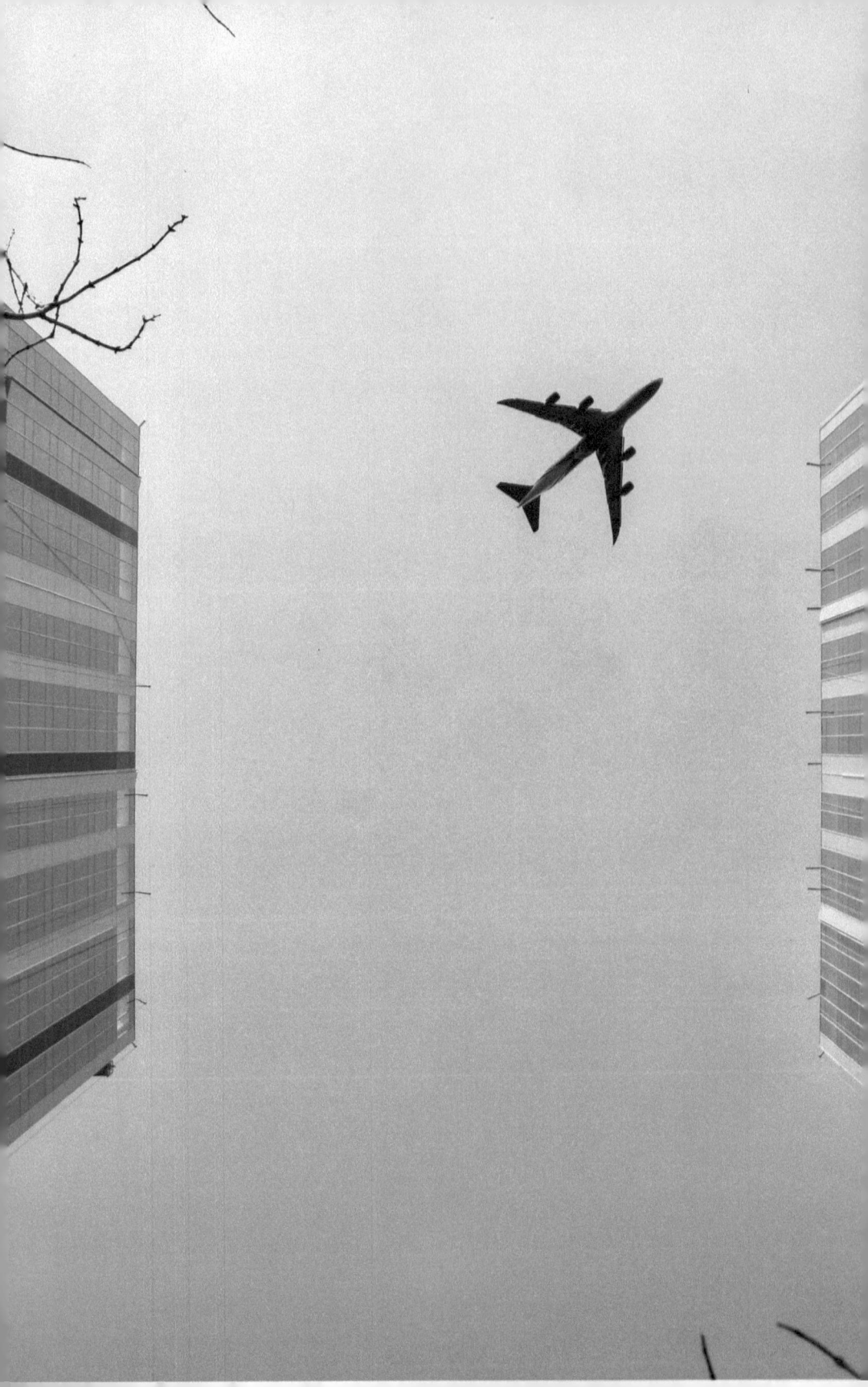

www.ingramcontent.com/pod-product-compliance
Lightning Source LLC
Chambersburg PA
CBHW021024180526

45163CB00005B/2097